I Believe in Me

Danielle Lundstrom

I Believe In Me
ISBN: 978-1-5272-8235-3

First published in Great Britain in 2020 through Amazon
self-publishing service Kindle Direct Publishing

Produced by samanthahoughton.co.uk

Content

Acknowledgments

I want to thank my mum for being beautiful inside and out, raising four children, giving us nothing but unconditional love. She put everyone else before herself and is just a real earth angel, with qualities and warmth like no other I know. Without my mum I would not be the understanding caring person I am today. My mum loved and cared for her beautiful father until he passed away at the age of 70. He was a beautiful person, I dream about him regularly and I know he is always with us in spirit; my mother misses him every single day.

I also want to thank my stepfather for loving my mum, for loving her kids like his own and for being the loving soul that he is. I could not ask for a more loving upbringing and I always say love is everything. I love my parents, I love my father, I love my father in-law as I have lived with him for half of my life. I always say I have three dads because I love them all unconditionally, for different reasons.

I love my in-laws, my mother-in-law and her children, so I am blessed with my mum as well as Rob's mum.

I love, accept and forgive my loved ones every five minutes because family means everything to me. You don't have to agree with how people behave but it does not stop you loving them.

I want to thank my brothers and sisters for all being so different but for all meaning just as much to me - I love you all!

I want to thank my Nan, granddad, and all the previous generations, all my loved ones here and in heaven. I love you all, miss you all and know you are around us - in my heart, thoughts and prayers.

I want to thank my (real) friends.

I want to thank my best friend, my life, my man, who is my everything; he is a wise, laid-back true soul, who is honest, and a hardworking, handsome, beautiful father of my child? 17 years stronger than ever. Without him I wouldn't feel as free as a bird, he loves me and all my imperfections, just like I love him. He is, as well as my son, the light of my life and the reason I feel complete.

I want to thank the people who have been there for me, the people who really care and understand me, for being just me.

I want to thank my friend Howard Davison with whom I have had many spiritual experiences, and the people I have met who give out such good energy, love and light.

Thanks Leanne (love & light) for your healing Reiki, messages and understanding. Thanks Emma L. Mather, who I have built such a good friendship with, for typing up this book for me.

How can I forget my beautiful child who is the most precious gift life has ever blessed me with, who has taught me more about myself in two years than life has ever taught me? I thought I knew it all until I became a mum but now I know what's important and what is not. Precious child of mine, I have so much to thank you for, you are my everything and all I love. Such an innocent, precious, delightful human being who I gaze at constantly. I love you, Son, with all my heart and soul

Most of all I would like to thank myself, my spirits, angels, spirit guides, energies, feelings, thoughts, my awareness and me for putting this pen to paper and writing my truth. I believe in me. I hope you enjoy. Cover design – Laura Brand and my sister Danica, who created the front cover picture of the unicorn and I.

Introduction

I am no master Buddha, Saint or God, but I am me and I believe in me. I believe I was meant to write my book and I feel it's happened for all the right reasons, and I know I have a message to get across. It might not suit everyone, but I have to follow my heart and go with what feels right.

I know that my purpose, is to help others, as it's something I've naturally done since I was a child. I believe I have awareness and the older and wiser I get, the more I step into the light and the more I help others in so many ways. I used to question my gift, but now I embrace it and even find myself healing people who hurt me, put me down or misunderstand me as I feel they need to be forgiven. I try to bring out the best in everyone, regardless. I feel blessed to share my thoughts, feelings and experiences in this book that I called 'I Believe In Me' because I do.

I believe we are all different, all unique and individual. I have spent my whole life soul-searching, trying to be a good person and I have found that we all make mistakes, have addictions and like nice things. It's OK to want nice things, but it's also more important to be grateful for everything you have got.

I believe I am writing this book because I cannot ignore what my heart is telling me to do; it feels so right, just like it feels right that I believe in who I am. I believe my book will help people to know they are not alone, and to open up and embrace where they are now so that they can grow and help others.

Chapter 1 - What I See, Feel and Think

I look around and I see most of the population moaning, complaining, and being ungrateful. I see selfish, needy, competitive humans trying to be better than each other, trying to find happiness in winning lottery money. Not many really stop for a second to see the beauty in life, to love and appreciate a moment, a new-born child, flowers, the sky, the stars, the universe, or how amazing life really is.

My purpose is to write my truth and help people understand that life is only as hard as you choose to make it. You are not a victim, none of us are, bad things happen to all of us, things go wrong without hard times how would we be grateful for the best times? Everything happens for a reason. We have to ride the wave, make life as smooth as we can for ourselves and others around us.

.Nobody means to be unkind in the end; they just don't know any different. We are all brought up differently by our parents, and to the best of their ability with the knowledge and understanding they had. Our parents did the best they could for us; they know only how they have been brought up, and we have to forgive people who hurt us. We have to forgive them because they will learn when the time is right for them. People claim they are right even if they are wrong. A person could swear something was black if it was white - It's only words. It's only what they believe, it doesn't matter what they think; what matters is what you know, you do not have to prove yourself to anyone. Your self-worth should be enough to know that anything you want is possible and that you should do whatever makes you happy.

I am my own best friend, I love myself deeply, I forgive myself every time I have done something wrong and I move on. I do not dwell in self-pity and I do not blame anyone but myself if I'm feeling down, weak, vulnerable or insecure - because I know not to depend on anyone but myself to make me happy. I love my partner 100% and he isn't perfect, like I am not. I forgive him for all his faults and I bring out the best in him even when he's not making me feel my best, because I don't depend on him to make me happy. I just expect respect and to be loved; that's all I ask. I love all his imperfections like I love mine. All is good in my thoughts, always, and that's how I choose to live.

Being a 24/7 full-time mummy, I get tired. I often feel like I'm doing everything on my own but my son is my life. I'm aware that if I complain about how hard it is being a mum, then I'm only going to find it harder. My son is two years old; not once have I complained, not once have I wanted a break or expected anyone to do my job, he is my life. If he's happy, then so am I, simple as. I get a million times back what I put in; time, patience and love. My son is loved, happy, and content and that makes me very proud indeed.

As long as we are doing our best, it's all we can do. Make every day count and make every moment count. Don't be hard on yourself because you think people are coping better or seem to be getting on in life while you're not. The less you complain the happier you will be. For every negative thought that comes into your mind, change it to a grateful, happy, positive thought and remember you choose your own thoughts; every thought you think is your own thinking. Change your way of thinking and watch everything around you change. Start by being grateful for everything you have, not what you don't have. Focus on your blessings not your problems. Practice every day to think happy thoughts until one day you will wake up and never want to complain again. Be positive and you're instantly being aware of any negative thoughts. Your life will change when you change the way you think.

I want to help people realise their worth. I want everyone to realise how amazing they are, and I want women to look in the mirror and realise they don't have to fix how they look on the outside, but find and have self-worth from the inside. Love yourself for who you are and know you are just as important as anyone else. You don't have to look a certain way or be a certain way to be accepted; you don't need anyone's approval but your own. Know that anything you want is possible. We can be successful in many ways, it doesn't mean you are famous, rich or good looking. I'd say success comes in many forms, such as having nothing and believing in yourself. These are things that can come from having no money, but also a knowledge that you can bring anything to your life through thought. There are lots of ways to be proud.

I always say not to change to try to make people like you. I always see in people what they don't see in themselves, such as strength and beauty. Also, I never judge a person by what they look like, I see into the soul, I see how I can help them. I feel why they are so lost and hard on themselves, and I know there are many reasons they choose to be hard on themselves. Then I try to remind them how amazing they are.

If we spent less time picking out our faults and more time realising how beautiful we are, then we could help others. I honestly believe the more you love and approve of yourself, then the more beautiful you grow. Shape, size, height and weight don't matter and it's normally ourselves who are most critical of ourselves.

How can we expect anyone to love us if we can't love ourselves? If we loved ourselves enough we really wouldn't need anyone else's approval. We live in a world of image and fakes, we feel we need to be or have a certain look to be accepted, but we really don't. We just need to accept ourselves from deep within and have fun along the way. I say do well, be good, feel good, say good and all will be good. Don't give to expect back, just give because you want to.

We should teach our children to be grateful; our children shouldn't have to feel pressured into having to look and be like everyone else. We are all different for a reason, we are not meant to be followers; we are born to be leaders, to live our own path, not everyone else's. We should not have to be accepted, we should accept ourselves and find self-worth so we can spread our own wings and fly.

I have always been my own person, I've never felt odd being completely unique; in fact, I love being different and I do everything on my own. I remember being really young and all my mates would be out; I'd be looking at four walls feeling blessed that I wasn't in a pub full of people with whom I had nothing in common with. People would be gossiping about others and I'd walk away and sit in my own thoughts. I was always aware that talking about others wasn't good; it's a waste of energy, time, and effort.

I just love being in my own space, I used to find myself drained a lot being a hairdresser but it was never exhaustion; it was picking up on bad, negative energies. I'd always find myself healing and helping most clients and I'd go home worn out, thinking, 'Why do people want to be so hard on themselves?' I'd wonder why anyone would want to make life harder than it already is. OK, so it's good to have a good old gab but people talk like they are so hard-done-by and really don't take a minute to stop, smile, breathe and just be grateful.

I see and meet so many people with everything money can buy, yet they are miserable. Then you find people with nothing who are so grateful. We need to realise we don't need material things and fancy cars to be happy, we don't need to bother impressing anyone, we just choose to. We live in a rat race but we can choose to be a rat or choose to run our own race, fast or slow. Nothing should be rushed; life is to be lived, so love every second, through good times and bad times. Take the good with the bad and know that something is on your side. Everything is sent to test you and the more we realise how amazing we are and trust in ourselves, the more life will prove to us how powerful, mind blowing and wonderful the world can really be. Choose how you look at life because how you choose to look at what's all around you is how it will choose to look at you.

I often meditate; I see only beautiful things. I see my world is beautiful because beauty is all I choose to see in my thoughts, dreams and meditation. I see my loved ones, angels, wings, beaches, sea waves, sand, beautifully fresh flowers, rainbows, yellow brick roads. I see white clouds and white horses, I fly on golden eagles, I look at castles in the land of pure delight. My mind has taken me to amazing places and I don't choose to be anywhere else because in my little bubble is where I'm most happy. It's easy to dwell on all the bad in the world but where is that going to get you? What good will complaining do? You are only upsetting yourself. You have to change in order to help others. How can you expect to grow and learn by being hard on yourself and on everyone around you?

I like to think I'm more than forgiving. I like to think I am an understanding person and that I don't judge anybody. I just like to help people, it is always in my attention to understand people the best I can, and simply forgive them because they will learn. Life really is so, so simple; we just choose to make everything so hard. My purpose is to write my book and if only one person understands it and it can change how they look at life, then I've done my bit and changed one person's life for the better.

I don't believe I am better than anybody else, in fact I find people amazingly interesting. If we could all see for ourselves, how good people are and value what others see, people would go from strength to strength in achieving greatness. Just think how wonderful the energy would be all around us if we saw the beauty in everything rather than complaining. Life became more beautiful to me, after my son was born. The miracle of a child is the best gift life could ever bless you with; to watch a child grow and learn is the most amazing thing to see. When a child has grown from a tiny seed to a human being, to see it learn to talk, walk, and grow is one thing, but the love you get back from a child is a million, worth everything you put in.

Being a mummy to me was like a walk in the park, even though it's the most consistently tiring job ever, I love it. How can you not love a child? Being a mummy has shown me how patient I am, how much I don't complain, how much I can give without expecting anything back. My son has taught me how strong I am. How happy I make him and how content he is makes me so proud. I can take him anywhere day in and day out. I never realised I could be so good at something; being a mum is the best but hardest job I've ever had to do. You don't clock off, but you get so much from it.

I really admire women. I thought I understood women until I became a mum. Mums are amazing, all women are something else. I love being a woman, I love seeing women happy and I love women who are proud and independent, but I want to help women who don't believe in themselves. I want them to look in the mirror and see what others see in them; beauty and strength so they know their worth. Never let the opinion of others affect how you feel as it's only an opinion, it's not the truth. If someone is unkind to you it's because they are choosing to be, it means nothing, what matters is how you feel about yourself and if you don't feel good then change the way you think because what you're choosing to think is choosing to make you feel down. That is not good because when you are down, you blame others and others aren't to blame. If you want someone to blame, blame yourself for being hard on yourself and everyone around you. The sooner you take action for your own thoughts responsibly, the sooner you can start improving your self-esteem.

Even the most confident of people need to practice daily how they think, act and behave. Even the most positive, happy-go-lucky people have hard times, sad times and bad times like the rest of us but it's how we deal with every situation that makes us who we are. If you don't appreciate anything or anyone, or what you already have, then how can you expect to be happy until you learn to be grateful? You may have to go without for months, years or forever but where will being miserable get you? Isn't it easier to be happy while you are here? Live, love, laugh, learn but most of all enjoy the moment, every moment, no matter what moment you are in. Make it special, make it happy and make a bad situation a better one, make an amazing moment an even more amazing one. Don't waste a moment bringing out the worst in someone. Bring out the best in everyone you meet, even if they don't bring out the best in you, do it to help others. They need it, we all need it.

The way I am, I can meet people from any walk of life
- it doesn't matter who you are, where you're from,
what you know or what you think - you know I will
treat everyone with respect and understanding. I
naturally heal people because I am naturally a nice
person and want to bring out the best in everyone.
Everyone has reasons for the way they are, some want
to be and do better; some just don't want to help
themselves at all. It's harder to help people who don't
want to help themselves, but know that in time they
will learn. One day we will all learn and we are all on
different levels. The trick is to help yourself in order
to help others and if they don't want advice, help or
guidance, then that's ok.

No one said life was going to be easy and no one said
life has to be made harder. We choose what we allow
into our life. Who said we had to live by a rule? No,
we don't have to follow any rules but to be good, do
good and see the good in all you do, then maybe, one
day, life will see the good in you. You can't just be a
good person for a day, a week or a month. You have

to be consistent in all you do. What is the point in pretending to be someone you're not? Why lie to yourself? It's pointless, meaningless and has no purpose. Be your true self, be who you want to be, not what you want others to see. Speak your truth, shine your light and if people don't like you, or themselves for that matter, then that's OK because they will learn. We have to allow everyone to live how they wish to live. We can't tell a person what's right for them because everyone has to do what they feel is right at the time. I often ask myself why I am so deep, why I can't just live every day without wondering why some things are just so wrong, but we have no control over others and all we can do is better ourselves.

Some people can live every day without a care in the world. I am the least heartless person. I am sensitive, emotional, kind, thoughtful and caring, but I've learned that emotions can get the better of us. We can't let feelings, emotions and heartless, rude, unkind, disloyal people stop us from believing in our self-worth and happiness. If I had a magic wand I'd take away all the hurt and suffering, and I'd want everyone to get along but life isn't that simple and we cannot change others, we have to start by changing ourselves.

I always say I need to just live, stop trying to help and understand people, but I will always want to help people, it's something inside me. I will never be perfect, but I will always grow, learn and have a heart of gold and feel for people.

Never make other people's business your business; it's ok to care but it's none of your business what they do. Keep life simple, drama free, stress free and as pleasant as you can, for it can be hard enough. I believe life is a battle for us all, we all have that little voice in our head we could call the devil then another which is your 'higher self', or 'angel guide' or God, whatever you may call it. I've always had the belief that someone or something is watching how we behave every second of every day, whether it's our higher self or whatever force it is. I know there is a power and a force that's powerful enough to take everything away from you at any time. I do believe that everything happens for a reason but I also believe we make our own choices.

None of us know what it's all about, as the big question is, 'What is it all about?' We can all dwell on why we are here, why life is so hard, why everything is so costly, why living is the way it is, why I can't have what he's got, or why bad people seem to get all the good come their way. The thing is they don't. They just claim that everything is good and life is rosy. But, that power known as karma can just come and wipe it all away from you. The cars, the materials, bricks, mortar, none of it means anything without love, gratitude and happiness. If you have found true happiness with nothing, then you are successful. If you can live every day with love, gratefulness and happy positive thoughts, then the day is worth living. What is the point in having all the money in the world, but no meaning, no lessons, no challenge, no love; just emptiness?

We have to find ourselves before we find money. I'd say to anyone looking to find themselves, not to dwell on what's gone, not to focus on trying to better your future, but to focus on the now. Do what can make you happy now, in this moment; love and respect everyone around you now. Now is every day and now makes everything. Now is not beating yourself up about yesterday or thinking about tomorrow, it's loving now. It's OK to have dreams, plans and lists, but don't be hard on yourself if things don't work out; just tell yourself that now I am loving this moment and that is all that's important. Practice to be present, to be blessed, to count your blessings every second of every moment, to respect everything and everyone. Life is a gift, cherish it, love it and learn from it.

Chapter 2 - Feeling Different –
Always the Dreamer

I always knew I was different; I was always aware at such a young age. I always wanted to better my life, always wanted to be independent and work hard. It almost felt like I had to prove my worth to people and be accepted but I don't know why. Of course I know now that none of that is important, but back then I almost felt like I must do well. I loved singing; I sung solos in every school play from junior to senior school. I took myself to many auditions because I thought I wanted to be Annie. I wanted to be seen and heard and was very loud. I sang all over the school playgrounds and wrote poetry in maths classes. I was always very artistic and loved performing even though my drama teacher had nothing in common with me, in fact it was clear I annoyed her and she never saw my potential or even wanted to.

My music teacher believed in me a lot. He loved my confidence and played the piano while I sang solos like 'Walking in the Air', 'Little Mermaid' and songs he'd written himself. I loved music, loved singing, loved poetry and loved writing songs. I have songs I've written as a young child and poetry - I have kept them. It's funny because when Jessie J brought her album out 'I'm Alive' most of the words in her songs I'd already written as a kid, like I'd written lots of books in my head. We are all powerful beyond measures; it's no secret, it's a fact. Life is what you choose to make it, simple as. Every thought as a child I brought to reality. I would dream I'd be in 'Annie' and 'Oliver' and I was one of the main orphans in both musicals we practiced away from home.

I was 11 years old and took myself to the auditions and all the rehearsals. I got to sing and dance in shows as a child. I'd dream of doing work as an 'extra' and appeared on Hollyoaks. I dreamed of working for top salons and worked for four as my hairdressing went from strength to strength. I now work for myself. I'd dream of spending the rest of my life with this beautiful man, and here I am years later in love and growing stronger every day. I planned to come off the pill when I was 30, weeks later I became pregnant and my child is a dream. I wanted to pass my driving test and

I did. I now have no car due to losing my license for speeding but everything happens for a reason, and I will tell you why later on, but if I still drove I wouldn't be writing this book. All the walking has inspired me a lot because I do a lot of walking; I tell you that for sure.

Who'd have thought I would be doing pageants at 33? I wanted to raise money for charity, doing something for a purpose and ended up winning three titles in one year with crows, sashes, medals, trophies, photo shoots, catwalks, fashion shows, runway; but none of it means more to me than what I am here to do and that is to help others. To speak out and share with others that anything is possible, anything can be achieved, you just have to believe. In my experience nothing comes easily; you have to know what you want, you have to believe that you Can and know that you Will. Do not let the distractions of others ever stop you.

To some, my dreams and goals may mean nothing, but to me I know how it's all come into my reality. I know you have to work hard for it but most of all be a good person. Not everyone will like you but not everyone matters and not everyone will understand you but it is ok. You must follow your dreams anyway. I've always been one for stepping out of my comfort zone. I get bored easily, learn quickly and move on. I'm so proud of who I am, I am proud of the knowledge and life skills I have that I can share with others, but mostly proud to be a hard-working mummy who, no matter how hard life gets, will fight for what she believes in.

Life is whatever you choose to make it. My advice would be to try to understand other people, try to understand they are not you, respect that they don't think like you and won't behave like you, so just be yourself and let others be themselves. Don't depend on other people to make you happy, don't feel pressured into trying to have a perfect life or be a perfect person because life isn't like that. Make life perfect for yourself because you will never be happy trying to be someone else. Don't rush life because you feel time is running out, everything happens in all the right time for all the right reasons.

I like to believe I've made a lot of really good choices and don't have regrets, but I also believe it's never too late to start changing, to start being good to yourself, and when things don't go your way or to plan, choose to be patient, not ungrateful. Being ungrateful will get you nowhere, I've always known that I want to live a happy, grateful life. I always wanted to be a hairdresser, work hard, be independent and to be a good person. I've always been grateful for having work, money and almost feel guilty that I am happy and others may not be. I've always been lucky enough to be aware that I can have, be or do anything I wish and that my life is in my hands. I believe that I've attracted everything to me by the way that I think. I also believe that every hard part in my life has been a lesson; everything that I've done wrong has made me realise what I can make right.

What we give out comes back to us, good or bad; it's how we deal with situations, and how we react to them, that is a reflection of us. We will learn, we are learning every day and I now believe my mindset is on another level. I used to always have goals, but they were only small goals like paying a debt this week, booking a holiday, having driving lessons or getting a car. Now my goals are more like writing a book, getting it published, making it a best seller and helping others to believe in themselves. I have so many dreams and desires because I have lived, loved, learned and experienced so much in my life that I do believe I have a gift and my gift is that I believe in me. I've helped so many people; I've seen people change their lives through my advice and guidance, I know people look up to me to follow their dreams. I don't believe I'm anything special or different. I just believe that I believe in myself and some don't or choose not to.

Everything life has brought to me has been through my own thought, actions and behaviour, FACT. I am very happy and proud that I am confident enough to help others. I know and believe that someone from any walk of life could sit next to me and I'd be able to help them in some way. One day I will be known as a healer, a self-helper, an adviser and my book will be a BEST SELLER. I know this because everything in life and every life experience challenge and problem that I've had to face, has made me the strong, independent, happy, confident person I am today. I hope my book will help and inspire people to believe they are amazing, beautiful and capable of anything. I hope the first person to read this feels inspired and it helps them. Everything I write is my truth, my beliefs, my story and what has helped me deal with day-to-day life.

I've woken up with an empty bank account, no money, no car and no job but I've made what seems a worst situation into the best place I could be right now, and that is content, and confident with what I've got. I know that hard times don't last forever, nor do good, but hard times make you stronger, more grateful and only get harder if you let them beat you. Know that any situation can be changed and in time all bad feelings will pass and everything is always good. Love, learn, be happy and breathe. Enjoy the sun, the sea's waves, light, love, happiness, joy, goodness, family, friends, good times and beauty. Life is a miracle; life is powerful, beautiful, interesting and challenging. Our future is us; we are the children's future. Teach them all good, teach them to be good and they will know only good. Who said they have to see bad? If your mind doesn't choose badly then all in your world is good.

When you sleep, rest, chill or meditate, think only happy, grateful, wonderful thoughts; think of things that make you feel good; plan your day to do things that you are grateful for; set yourself goals that you'll be proud of achieving, that make you proud of who you are. Don't compete, don't compare yourself and don't wonder why others have things that you don't. These things that aren't real, THEY ARE JUST THINGS; be real, give love, do good, feel good, see good, smile, be happy, help and enjoy. Treat yourself, don't be hard on yourself, you're worth more than that. Whatever situation you are in, make it work, fight for it, if it's worth fighting for.

Don't try to fix what's not broken. Don't push loved ones away because you think they don't love you enough - love YOURSELF first so that you can help them. Maybe they can't love like you, maybe they were not shown love. Work at what you want; bring out the best in everyone you meet; be nice, smile, show love and respect. The kinder you are to yourself and others, then the kinder life will be to you. If things aren't going your way, look in the mirror, change how you feel about yourself, approve of yourself. Love yourself; you are more than worth it. Where does hating yourself get you? There is no better feeling than the feeling of being grateful for everything. I am grateful for when times get hard as well as when they are going really well. I like to think that when you are going through really hard times, you have to know that it will all pass and by worrying, dwelling, beating yourself up - it won't make anything go away. In fact it will bring more worry.

If however you remain positive, always, then you will see the light at the end of the tunnel. It's all down to you. Your attitude, gratitude and behaviour all change your life; it either makes you or breaks you. I know this because I have experienced it and I've been positive about everything for as long as I can remember. Only now, it is all I am.

I live, breathe, and know nothing other than to be positive about everything, no matter what; a feeling will pass, and bad times don't last forever. Life tests us, it makes us, breaks us, but I tell you one thing and that is once you are down, there is only one way you can go, that is to learn from it and get right back up.

Chapter 3 - Focus on the Good

I am the type of person to have nothing and make everything from it. I focus only on the good every second of every day and I do not give up on myself. I get what I want and what I feel I deserve. I have massive worth and I deserve everything that comes to me, good and bad, because everything happens for a reason. I have dreams and was born to make them a reality; I will, because I believe I can. There is nothing more rewarding in life than feeling blessed, feeling joy. I love the feeling of happy times, happy moments, and happy memories. We really need to count our blessings more and be grateful for what we have that others don't. I am no different from anyone else, I've just programmed my mind to be thankful for literally everything and it works for me.

I could write a list of things I have to complain about like people; people can make life so annoying but only if you let them. People blame everything but themselves for literally everything, when they forget it's their own mind draining itself. You are your own worst enemy; you have to control your own state of mind in order to feel grateful - once you're grateful you are happy. I know that most of us are critical towards ourselves, that most of us would rather pick out faults in ourselves than recognise our qualities that make us who we are. I know that none of us are perfect and I certainly don't claim to be perfect either, but why not learn to love all our imperfections, learn to love who we are, not beat ourselves up about who we could be and should be, because, believe it or not, once you learn to love and accept yourself for who you are, then you learn to love all your wrinkles, your scars, all your marks, your freckles. If you love yourself whatever shape, size, height, weight you are, then your beauty grows. It grows from in and out because you no longer care what people think. Go out without your make-up on, not looking your best - so what! Why do you care what others think? As long as you're happy, that is all that matters.

One day I learned just to love myself even on days I looked pale and drained, even when I've not had the money to look my best. I find when you can't have money or material to cover how you feel, it makes you love yourself even more. If you love yourself from deep within, then it doesn't matter what you wear, who you hang out with, what car you drive, how much money you've got or what job and promotion you have. It all comes from within and you don't need things to cover up how you feel, you need to feel good without things.

One thing I always knew at a young age was never to be a sheep. People would say to me, 'Why aren't you married? Why don't you have your own house? Why haven't you got children yet? Your worth more than that, blah, blah, blah...' I never once took any notice. No-one has the right to tell you how you should be living your own life especially when the people telling you need to take a good look in the mirror. There is a difference between people being nice and people talking for the sake of it, so never listen to anyone but your inner self. Do what makes you happy, not what pleases others. If you like to impress others you will never feel complete. Give yourself some credit, give yourself a pat on the back, just for being you and getting this far in life. Forget about the past, about dwelling on what you've said, done or could have changed. Move on, let go, set yourself free from drama, negativity and start today, start now. Look in the mirror and tell yourself you are really worth being good to.

Be good to yourself, love yourself, and value yourself, have self-worth because you are the most important person in your life; realise that if you are not happy, it's only because of yourself. Never blame others for how you feel because that is a selfish act, it makes you weak and you are not weak. Forgive people who have hurt you, let go and move on; start all over today, make everything better today, tell people you care, forgive them, hug them, and be nice to them. They need it, just like you do; we all need to be loved and understood, it's the only way to live happy and free. Next time a critical negative thought comes into your head about you or anyone else, let it go, please. Think only happy, positive, grateful thoughts; life is too short and precious to be hard on yourself. You must forgive every day, you must love every day, you must learn every day in order to grow, because it makes you a better person to do good. Being a better person makes you feel happy, while blaming everything and everyone around you only makes you unhappy.

Life is what you choose it to be, I could list a million things that I don't like in others or that I don't agree with, but I choose to focus on what I have got and what good I can make out of each situation. I choose not to be a victim and although I am not going to lie to myself and say my life is perfect, I make everything I have got, perfect for me. I make life as pleasant as I can for the people I choose to spend my time with and I walk away from drama. I do not gossip, I don't spend time around people I don't like and if something doesn't feel right I move on. I do not wish to make people's business my business, no matter who they are or how close I am to them. I have very few friends and despite the fact I love my family, every single one of them, I never get involved in their business.

I say we all learn in life and we all make our own choices. We all have our own minds, we all choose how we act, behave and live, and no one but ourselves can free our own mind. I don't believe everyone has mastered everything and has the answer to every question, but I do believe some people, like myself, have a good understanding, a deeper awareness so they can help others who don't understand or who can't grasp that life really is simple. We just choose to make everything so much harder and more complicated than it really is. I'd say to just live simply, live gratefully, forgive and learn. If we learn from our mistakes, then we are learning lessons and growing from them.

The reason I am writing this book is because I believe not everyone has a good understanding about life and not everyone chooses to. Some people are happy living to be ungrateful and miserable, complaining a lot, never being satisfied and claiming everything is ok when, deep down, they are lying to themselves. None of us are perfect and we all choose to live how we wish to live, like I choose to be true to who I am. I have always believed in having my own mind, being my own person and going by what I believe in. I believe in myself, and I believe that I am meant to write this book to help people understand that life doesn't have to be hard. Life is a choice, we attract what we choose to think and we feel what we choose to dwell on. No-one is better than anyone else; we are all amazing, we are all born to enjoy the beauty of life, not what we believe to be true by listening to other people's opinions. We have our own beliefs to be guided by, from our own experiences; who made the rule up that we have to live by a rule or by how others live? Who said we have to have the perfect life, with marriage, children, cars and fancy houses? None of this means anything so why live to impress and why not impress yourself instead, by doing it for you!

Start by believing in yourself, finding self-worth, not depending on people or fancy things. Instead, look into your soul, ask yourself who you are and what you want, then, go and make it happen. Rather than saying you want to lose weight, go and do it, make it happen. Rather than saying you want a holiday, go and book it, make it happen, you can pay for a holiday if you can afford junk food, crisps, alcohol or drugs.

You can change, you have the choice, you either choose to make things happen and get things done, or you choose not to. If you choose to stay in a rut, then you cannot blame anyone else but yourself for staying in it. Nothing beats the truth, and if you can take criticism and grow from it, then that's good. If your partner doesn't want what you want, or support you in what you want, then that doesn't mean they don't care about you, you have to do it for yourself, make it happen, because you want to and you don't need anyone's advice or encouragement, they are not you. All you must do is believe that you can make anything happen.

I hope this short book can help others realise their worth, know that they are amazing but most importantly know each and every one of us has the power to make anything happen. If you aren't getting results, answers or evidence then maybe you want it too much. Maybe you are looking too hard and maybe you need to live your life being more thankful for the simple things you already have. Start with baby steps, as you must crawl before you can walk and you must walk before you can learn to fly. If you are genuinely grateful for every second of every day, no matter what or who you're with and how much money you have (or haven't) then you will be happy. To be happy, you have to love yourself from deep within, you have to love and forgive everyone including yourself, no matter what. Being happy isn't something you can fake because you cannot lie to yourself, as you'd only be hurting yourself. Once you are at total peace with yourself then that's when you are flying without wings. All bad becomes good, all ugly becomes beautiful, all dark becomes light and then life becomes worth living.

When you love yourself, you can help others and when you help others it feels good. When others learn from you, then you know you have a purpose and that is your gift to the world, it's yourself.

All I know, is that I believe my own truth because I have lived it, experienced it, learned from it and grown from it. By 'it' I mean life, my inner self, spirit guides, knowledge, and understanding. I've experienced enough to write my own truth, and from this I will grow and continue to help others. I have a solid, healthy, happy, relationship, a beautiful contented child who is my whole life, and I have amazing supportive in-laws and family who I love with all my heart. My brothers and sister mean everything to me, my mum is my inspiration, my role model, the wind beneath my wings and I have so many people I'd be nothing without.

I've been hurt, lost, undiscovered and misunderstood; I've felt lost, lonely, unloved and alone. But I'm strong, independent, hardworking, and I know my worth. I love myself, believe in myself and I don't think I am better than anyone else. I just believe there is something amazingly wonderful about this world we live in and we've been given an opportunity to love it, respect it, learn from it, be grateful for it, grow from it, believe in it and achieve anything we deserve, because we all have it in ourselves, to see beneath our beautiful selves to get from this life what we deserve. I can honestly say I don't believe that the grass is ever greener on the other side, but I do believe we waste too much time thinking it is, rather than watering our own seeds and growing, learning and knowing that no one has a perfect life. People just choose to make it as perfect as they can, because that is how we grow to know that it is just what it is, simple as. That is why some people with money and everything, aren't necessarily happy because they haven't found themselves before they have found or attracted money. I've had a positive state of mind for as far back as I can remember; I have planned what I want by writing it down or thinking about it, then letting nothing stop me in achieving it. I've always worked hard for everything and never expected anything from anyone, or for anyone to do it for me. I've brought to my reality: holidays, cars, jobs, promotions, anything I've dreamed of, I've made things happen in my life, and so can you.

I live day by day, taking the good with the bad, but I try to do my best and make every second of every day count. I have goals, dreams, ambitions and I don't let money or bad situations take over my positive state of mind. My mindset is now on a level it's never been because I have thought I knew it all, had it all taken away from me, learned from it and got on with it. I am me and I don't claim to be anything I am not. I'm in a good place because I have been through hard times, been in dark holes and I have everything money can't buy - my health, family, happiness, my life lessons, knowledge, skills and self-worth.

Teach your children to love. Teach them to give love, to not want or need, but to love life – teach them to simply love being and show respect to others so they can teach their children. I am at a point in my life now where I just want to live and not think. I just want to enjoy moments and make every second count. I want life to be as pleasant as it can be for myself and the people I love around me. I now accept people's faults, no matter how much they've hurt me; I forgive, let go, move on and know the same people will hurt me again, but only if I choose to let them.

We have to accept that people are all different, people learn at different times and in different ways.
Some choose not to learn, others choose to grow and learn by their mistakes while others keep making the

same mistakes, and never see what they are doing. Never let a person drain you, as they may not ever change, but you can choose not to let them affect you. I want to now live with a clear mind, full of light, love, growth, passion and purpose. I have no time for nonsense, drama, bullshit and time wasters. Life is too short, precious and hard enough; worry, stress and dwelling on things that we cannot change is a waste of energy. Many of us spend too much time taking life for granted and disrespecting those around us without even thinking for a minute that before we know it, we have spent so much time complaining that we have forgotten how to live.

Living in my eyes is loving life, loving every moment, loving everyone around us and loving ourselves from deep within. It's about being grateful for things that money can't buy like friends, family, loved ones, trees, plants, animals, the sea, the sun, the moon, planets, stars, the sky, energy, spirit guides, the universe, food, water, shelter and things that so many of us take for granted. We really forget how lucky we are and forget to thank life for the simple things. It's not necessarily material things, cars, money or power that makes us grow; it's lessons, understanding, growth, love, and how we treat others and ourselves. It's how you look at life, how you choose your life to be and what you put into life that dictates what you get back. Okay, so bad things happen to us all; we get hurt, we suffer, we win or lose and people get taken away from us resulting in us becoming angry, bitter and hurt. It can make us stop believing due to a loss of faith in life or in ourselves. But, how can you expect to see the beauty of life when you choose to hate everything and everyone?

Love is the greatest power of all; love can heal anything; love and understanding will get you through anything. We may never know why bad things happen and why loved ones are taken away from us, but isn't it better to believe? Isn't it better to believe in love, peace and good things like rainbows, blue skies, blue birds, unicorns, light, stars, magic, passion, clouds, blue seas, creations, a new born child, a beautiful butterfly, the air we breathe, everything life has to offer us? Even how the human body works, how our hearts beat and how our minds work? Our mind can create wonders; it can turn dreams into reality. With our minds enlightened, we can move mountains, fly planes, achieve anything. Miracles happen and love is the most powerful energy we can give. If everyone loved, then just think how peaceful life would be without hate, anger, bitterness, jealousy, selfishness, needs, wants and competitions.

If we all had more understanding that life doesn't have to be as hard as we choose to make it, then this world would be so much easier to live in. It might not necessarily be easy and people can be difficult, life can be difficult, but it's about finding peace within. We need to be making peace with the things that cannot be changed, so instead change the mind-set on how you perceive life to be for yourself in order to be at peace with it. I like to think I have a great outlook on life, I don't believe I am perfect but I try my best to make every second of everyday count, and respect everyone around me. I forgive those who don't treat me as nicely as I treat them, or at least in my heart that is what I try to do. I bless them, and thank God I have more of an understanding and that I'm not as lost, hurt, angry or bitter as some people. Some people like to think they are a victim and that life has got it in for them, but the truth is they have got it in for themselves because they choose to blame everyone but themselves for being unhappy. Happiness is a choice, it is a fact.

If only we could live life without pretending, love without expecting and understand without taking offence. If only we could be happy and grateful without looking good, but feeling good instead. Don't live to impress others, but impress yourself; spend less time talking about others and focus on improving your own life rather than trying to outdo others. You will not achieve anything by having an ego. You may gain money, fame, or materials, but that won't buy you happiness, it will just cover up for how incontinent you really are on the inside. If you don't work on what's important for you rather than others, then you will never truly be happy. Let go of that ego, meditate, breathe, relax, enjoy the simple things, and love the people that love and respect you. Don't dwell on how others treat you or behave towards you, as they may not want to change. You however, can change, by just loving life, loving oneself, loving nature and simply being grateful not hateful. Be consistent in every area of life. Doing well and being good is all you can do.

Chapter 4 - Taking the Good Even From the Bad

It's all new beginnings for me from here; I am 33, and my book is written. I've spent most of my life soul searching, being nice to others, getting hurt, not feeling appreciated and questioning why others can be the way they are, but I now know that ok, I am free, and most of all I'm happy. I love myself deeply so I can help and understand others. I love my life, I am grateful for literally everything: for water, shelter, food, the air I breathe, my sense of smell, how my body works, my heart that beats, my feet that allow me to walk, my eyes that allow me to see, the people I meet, the places I go, the lessons I learn and how I grow.

I am grateful to the people who hurt me, and that's shown me who I don't wish to be. I'm grateful for the pain I've suffered; it has made me stronger than ever and by going through the hardest times of my life it has made me so grateful. I know that everything passes and doesn't last forever, just like the good things don't. We have to take the good with the bad, we have to be strong and we have to thank life for everything in order to grow from it. I now want to love my beautiful life in a way I've never loved it before, with more strength and knowledge than I've ever had. I want to grow, loving every second of my life and the people in it. I have always been happy but I now just want to live and not question, just simply be, and to enjoy what the rest of my life has to offer.

Life is short, precious and, as much as I say I don't complain and that I am grateful no matter what, I also believe in improving day by day. Even the wisest, who claim they have mastered everything, haven't. I always say it is best to grow and learn, than slip and keep making the same mistakes. I am at a point in my life where if the good things come along then so be it. I don't expect anything; I just live gratefully, happily and as pleasantly as can be. I try to make everyone around me happy, even if they aren't in happy moods; I would rather bring them up. I believe I am very patient and if things don't go my way, I make the most of what I've got even if it seems like nothing. It's everything to someone with nothing.

I used to live my life thinking we needed clothes, holidays and fancy things, but in all honesty I am more grateful coming home out of the cold to a nice warm tea and a bath, just to have shelter and the love from family. I like to plan nice things and enjoy life but I go without other things to get it. I do believe you can bring anything to you, but I also believe you should think whether it's important enough to you. Is it worth risking other things for and will you be hurting other people along the way? I believe in being a good person because even if others hurt you, at least you can sleep at night knowing you don't go out your way to hurt other people and bring others down, just for your own happiness. I like to live by the truth, so to write a book that had no truth in it would be pointless to me. But, to follow my heart and be really honest in writing means I am being honest to myself. With honesty comes truth and to be real makes it easier for me to express myself, which is why I believe I have learned so much and have a lot of knowledge at 33 years old.

I could easily make this book sound clever and complicated but that means only a few would understand it, and I'm not writing it to impress anyone but simply to just help. I do intend to write more as I have so much going on in my head daily, but this is simple, easy to read and hopefully people who choose to complain a lot may have more of an understanding, like I understand that we all hurt, suffer, feel pain and question life. However, my book is to help people make the most out of this short precious life we do have because we only get one shot. Life for me has so many lessons and so many things to learn. I've grasped a lot in my short life but others grasp a lot more; others, not much at all. My goal in life now is to write at least one or two more books and maybe speak out on stage, helping others have a better understanding. I am no fairy godmother and I cannot heal the world, but if I can help even one out of a hundred, then that will help them learn. When you learn you grow, when you grow, you can help others make the world a more pleasant place.

Be yourself, do what makes you happy, learn from your mistakes, take each day as it comes, live in the moment but take nothing for granted. Love yourself, respect yourself, be kind to yourself, be good to others, understand them, understand yourself, and don't be hard on yourself. Don't be unkind to other people, live a life of love, gratitude and learn every day to be a better you. Reach for the stars, follow your dreams, have goals, make plans, but don't be disappointed if things don't work out. Try new things, meet new friends, walk away from those who don't deserve you; live, learn, let go, move on, don't dwell. Every day is a new day to change your mindset, know that anything is possible and give life all that you have got. Don't waste life being ungrateful, hard on yourself or putting others down. Take a vacation, have a break, break the rules, live, smile, sing, dance, make love, walk in nature, breathe in life, get some sea air, clear your head, get rid of old clutter, get 'to do' lists done, feel productive, make the most of each day, make every second of every day count. Spend time with your loved ones and if you can't be with them then let them know you care. Say kind words, think nice thoughts, do nice deeds, know that there is heaven here on earth. Choose to make life beautiful, choose to see beauty in all you do, choose to be you. Inspire others, lift others up and don't let life kick you down. Be strong, be bold, be wise, and fight for what you believe in. Don't try to be anybody else but yourself, be your true self, grow into your higher self, spread your wings and fly. But most of all, do what makes you happy because you deserve it.

Know that life is always on your side if you are patient enough to understand it and work it all out. When you give up on life, it shall give up on you. When you stop believing, that is when you stop any good from coming into your life. Have faith, hope and courage. Be kind, show love, feel love, be free, don't give to expect but believe good is always on your side. Beauty is all around you, magic is everywhere. You just have to breathe, relax and know that when you are truly grateful for life it has wonderful ways of paying you back. When you choose to be happy, life brings you happiness. When you choose to not dwell, then life starts to remove all the worry from you.

When you choose to walk away from drama, then life brings you peace and contentment.

It's all simple - we just choose to think it's not. If we put as much effort into our self-worth and beliefs as we do our doubts and fears, then amazing things start to happen. Please believe this has worked for me. Don't give up on yourself because of a few life knock-backs and a few self-doubts. Look in the mirror today and make that change. Love the person you are, believe in you, love all your mistakes, forgive yourself, let go, move on, look into the eyes of the people that matter and tell them they matter before it's too late. Life is far too short, please start to love it, love those around you and be thankful that you are alive, including with what you have even if it seems like nothing. Write a list of everything you are grateful for and if you can't be grateful, then you need a lot of help. Start with small steps and improve your self-worth. Live for today, live everyday like it's a celebration. You don't need an excuse to be happy, just be happy. You don't need money to go on long walks or enjoy life; you don't need to explain to anyone why you want to step out of your comfort zone, just do it. Walk free, breathe in life, take time out, and bring out the best in the people you are around, because life can be hard enough. Let's make it pleasant and, hey, let's just simply be!

I like to think I am the easiest going, most laid-back person with a heart of gold, who is a free spirit and likes to make everything in life simple. I don't like to put myself on anyone; I am very independent and like to do everything myself. I love my own company and I don't expect anything from anyone. I have my little boy with me 24/7; he is my life, the best gift life has ever blessed me with. He is two years old and has taught me more in two years than anything in life ever did. I used to think I knew it all but now I know that he is all that matters and that life simply is what you make it. Writing a book doesn't make me any more important than anyone else but I believe everything in life has brought me here because this is what I am meant to do. My purpose is to help others; I believe we all have different qualities. Some people are beautiful inside and out; they just don't know it.

Some people have so much to learn and some live to actually believe they know it all, I'm just here to write from my heart and continue to be a better person each day. I've always gone out of my way to be nice to others and I've never understood why others can be so unkind, but if everyone was as nice as me then I wouldn't feel so blessed.

It takes every kind of people to make what life's about and it takes real passion, self-belief to put pen to paper and write my truth. I am a natural healer, I give naturally, good comes to me always and when bad things happen I learn from it. No one's life is perfect but I believe that, in life, we are given a choice to make; we can either choose to be a victim or choose to take the good with the bad and ride the wave of life the best way we can. Everything happens for a reason and loved ones are all around us, life is beautiful and it does not have to be hard, we just choose to make it. Just think how peaceful life would be without humans blaming everyone but themselves. I've always known that life is what you make it, it was in me to be a free spirit from as far back as I can remember. I've always known what is good for me and what isn't. Some people take longer to learn than others and some people never learn.

I say we all get the same 24 hours in a day; it's what you choose to do with that time. I've always known what I want and it was never to have money, because I always thought it was a selfish act, so I spent most of my life trying to do good instead. I've got a lot back from life, in fact, being a good person has answered all of my dreams because I have everything I've ever wanted that money can't buy. I have learned the hard way, that getting what I want isn't important but having everything I need is. I am not saying I've not had things that cost money, as I used to think I had to work really hard for money to make me happy, but now I know if I live by being true to who I am, then everything will come to me, because I strongly believe that being me has brought me right where I belong and here my book starts.

I have achieved a lot in my short life and to some people it might mean nothing but to me it means everything. I now know that staying real, being true, loyal, kind and honest is the best way forward. Even if you think people have more than you, they really don't and they will never be you, so stay true to who you are. Do what makes you happy, and if loving nature is more important to you than loving material things, then do that. We all like different things and what makes one person happy could be another person's idea of boredom, so each to their own.

Chapter 5 - This Is Me

My name is Danielle; I am 33 years old, a mother to a beautiful two year old boy who is the love of my life and the best thing that has ever happened to me. I have been with his daddy more than half of my life; he is my best friend, a beautiful wise soul who I love and respect with all my being. I have the most beautiful mother who is so caring, kind, thoughtful; she has taught me the greatest gift in life. That lesson is love, and even if you have nothing but love, you can get through anything. I love my family, my life, living, learning and growing. I love people and I learn so much from people but I like to think I am a free spirit. I do mostly everything on my own, love my own company and find myself healing and helping people daily. In my job I meet people from every walk of life. Because of the person I am, I seem to attract very interesting people and I learn something new everyday. I do pick up energies, so I can be instantly drained by negative energy; that's why I choose to either walk away, or help the person to try to think differently.

I have learned though, that you can't change others, but you can help yourself become a better person daily, and you will be forever learning no matter how much you think you know. I am simply me, just trying to do my best and I like to think I am at a point in life where it is what it is. I feel I've enough knowledge and life experiences to help others as much as I can. This does not mean I know everything or that I am implying that, but I am saying I have had a lot of experiences to be able to help another, where I may be able to help and give guidance. I am a hairdresser but I see myself more as a free spirit with a love for life, people and experiences. I've been hairdressing since a very young age, it's what I am good at and I've always had natural people skills. Hairdressing includes key communication skills and with working in all the top salons since leaving school, I'd say hairdressing started me off on a perfect career path from day one. I did two weeks' work experience at the age of 14; I remember being very keen, hardworking and more than interested. I was really good with people, really hands-on, going out my way to help all of the staff and learn as much as I could.

Even at just 14 I knew I wanted more from life but never really knew exactly what. I was given a job as a Saturday girl after a fortnight's work experience and had a Saturday job until I left school. I then went straight into college from school, training to be a hairdresser. My first placement was a local salon; I learned a lot, but soon enough I knew I wanted to be in the city where I'd be more hands-on, rather than just washing hair, sweeping floors, and pleasing people. I wanted to learn more, had itchy feet, hadn't qualified in college and still had loads to learn. But, I took myself into town and with my cheeky confidence, including people skills; I walked up to the reception and asked whoever was on the desk if I could speak to the big boss. I knew with me being in the middle of my training that it would be a bit awkward but I needed to take the step. Soon enough, I was working for Voodou on Bold Street and it was the best move I had ever made. Such a busy salon full of character, charm, fun and excitement, with thirty staff all unique in their own way. It was like it was meant to be and working at this cool place brought out all my confidence, friends and people skills.

I was promoted straight away to head assistant. At 17, that was a cool role to have with the extra money, extra responsibility. I was in charge of all the other assistants, making sure the salon was spotless, was on the ball, and anyone who worked with me will tell you how well I ran that place. I won an award for being the most helpful hands-on assistant to ever work at Voodou, Liverpool. Soon enough I was applying colours, washing, blowing hair and waiting on the clients, making them comfortable. I was practically running the stylists' column, only I wasn't qualified on paper. I was however, making the salon a good few bob and was itching to have my own clients and earn my own wages. I just had to be patient until my boss was ready to let me free on my own customers; it was then I learnt patience and unfortunately, you can't always have what you want and things take time; I always knew my worth, I just had to wait for the right time. Soon enough I was running my own column then was promoted to be a senior stylist. I'd work until seven at night then do mobile clients after work - I loved being busy and loved how, because I had a wage, I could book holidays, have driving lessons and buy clothes. Now I am a mum, that's all changed, but none of its important - I'll go into that later.

After many years of working at Voodou, with great people, from all walks of life, getting their hair done, I've developed great people skills and great communication. I learned a lot about myself and what I was capable of when I put my mind to it. I wasn't just a hairdresser, I was a great people person who listened, healed, understood others and could provide a service for them doing any type of haircut, colour or style; I felt like a life coach! We would sell retail, have targets to hit, work non-stop without a break. Natural talent is a gift and to have regular clients coming to the salon just to see you feels good. To be a natural people person is even better, because your clients love coming to you and you have that gift to make them feel very special.

Eventually, I got itchy feet; I was feeling taken for granted and I felt I was working very hard, but whilst I used to skip to work, I began to feel drained going in. My granddad was poorly and I just wanted to be with my family. I'd take my clients to the middle floor for some peace and I'd look at the clock, waiting to finish, I'd lost all my passion, strive and respect for the people I was working for. I wrote a letter explaining how I felt and that I just needed to be around my loved ones. I knew I was losing something good, walking out of such a great salon, but it felt right to do so. Since leaving Voodou, I've achieved more than enough and I have never looked back, but I loved every second of it and could write a book just on the whole experience.

My granddad was poorly and in hospital for eighteen weeks; I went to the hospital day and night because he meant that much to me and my mum. I walked out of my job leaving them a note saying I wanted to spend time with my beautiful granddad because I knew it felt right; I knew he was poorly and he needed us by his side. Leaving the salon where I'd worked for eight years was the best move I had made; spending my days with the bravest, strongest, most amazing man I loved and will never forget because I know he's all around us every day. I did a car boot sale to make some money and bought my first book called The Gift. I read it in the hospital next to my granddad, holding his hand, making sure he knew my mum and I were with him all the way. The book talked about a woman who claimed to have powers. Everything she talked about I understood, and I still believe to this day that this book was sent to me to let me know I had a gift myself; because I'm forever healing people, helping people, and I just knew my granddad wanted to pass over. He was just 70, he was an independent, beautiful, kind man who had an illness but never liked to complain. He had lost his legs but carried on. My mum adored her dad, he was her world, my granddad just seemed to bounce back from every fall, even after a kidney transplant and many other health problems. He was a fighter, but this time he caught MRSA in the hospital and his body just couldn't fight it; he'd had enough. I knew I had to be with him, so for 18 weeks I spent as much time as I could in that hospital and don't regret a second.

My granddad is one of the very special people in my life, and reading that book in the hospital gave me awareness, it made me realise I wasn't strange and that I had a gift. I don't like to go around saying I read minds as I think we all have awareness; we are all on different levels but I really do believe life is beautiful and that my granddad is all around us. Life is what you choose to make it, what we put in and how we see life is our own choice. I choose to believe in all good, kind, beautiful, happy, joyful, positive and blissful feelings. I don't like to think about any negative, draining, down, sad or bad feelings; I like to focus on what I want from life and do what makes me happy. I spent years trying to please others and I could never understand how some people could be so unkind, rude, ignorant, and hurtful. I realised we live in a world full of hate, drama, negativity, violence, bitterness, envy, jealousy and cruelty - but we don't have to focus on any of that, because we have a choice. We can walk away from drama and we don't have to listen or take notice of people being unkind. I live my life in pure bliss, happiness, peace and contentment with no drama, no hate and no bad energy. I choose to stay out of people's business because it's not my business.

I find myself helping people every day, healing others and naturally being a good soul. I am not one to mope or complain, and I do everything to make each day count. As much as I believe that the simple things in life mean so much, I still strive to do well and challenge myself; I am already writing a second book in my mind. I believe in guides, spirits, angels, a higher self, energies and all that is beautiful. I also believe all of this good stuff has brought me right to this moment where I put my pen to paper and help others. I want to write more books and speak out to people who don't have much of an understanding about how simple it can be to change your life by changing the way you think, act and behave, and by what you choose to believe in. People say silence and peace of mind is good; fair enough, it is, but, I believe it is good to also have fun and a sense of humour to speak out and help others if the words you are using are not unkind. If you are bringing out the best in everyone around you, then go ahead, speak your truth and let no one dull your shine. Do what you feel is right, do good, give good, be good, sing, dance, smile, laugh and don't hide how you feel. Let it all out and be able to express yourself. Follow your dreams, be proud of who you are and be your own kind of beautiful.

I want nothing more than to write more books, I have written in my diaries since way back. Everything I have brought into my life has been through thought, from writing down what I want from life, which I believe has brought me right to what I am doing now and that is writing my book. I would like to thank you for taking the time to read my book 'I Believe in Me!' I do hope you enjoy reading it. I work, look after my son, come home, shut my door and thank my lucky stars for the beauty of life, my son, man, in-laws, mum, brothers, sisters, family and all my loved ones. I let them all live how they choose to live and I do not judge; none of us are perfect, we all have to live, learn, make mistakes and move on; but the love I feel for my family is massive, they mean so much to me.

Every thought that goes through my head every minute of every day is a grateful, happy, loving thought of how blessed I am to have such a beautiful child, beautiful partner and how my mum is such a beautiful person with so many amazing qualities she could pass on to me.

I have lovely people around me and not a day goes by when I don't thank life for all I have. I've always had the awareness that people with money, power and cars, seemed to have it all but aren't necessary happy. I don't know what it is but I never envy anyone because I know we are all human and we are all just learning. With or without money you should be the same person, but I often think that if you have been handed it all on a plate, you will never learn the value and you will never feel as proud as you would earning everything yourself. There's no better feeling than having nothing and making everything you've ever wanted come to you through hard work, passion, commitment, strength and belief. Success isn't about making money, it's about being proud of who you are, knowing you have your own mind and going to sleep at night with your soul at peace. Knowing you give good to the world and do all you can to make the world a better place.

I am hoping this book helps people believe in themselves, to not be ashamed of who they are and know that it's ok to make mistakes but to move on and learn from them. Live in the moment, love every second of life and be grateful for every life experience. Rather than wanting someone else's life, focus on your own happiness. Focus on what you do have, not what you don't, and never take a second for granted. Think about it for a minute; you cannot buy love and the people in your life, so why push them aside or put them last to chase money, fame and power? It won't make you happy; if you can't find happiness with nothing, then you will never be happy because you are not truly grateful if you need money to make you happy.

Since becoming a mum, I now know how to go without; I know how being patient, positive, grateful and happy - no matter what - is worth more than any piece of clothing, car, home or pot of gold. Nothing else matters than the love you have for a child. The lessons you learn from becoming a mum make you a better person than you'll ever be. You learn to take the good with the bad and you feel more proud when you've achieved things than you ever otherwise would, as time is precious and patience is strength. You find strength to be a perfect mum - it's certainly something to be proud of - and the best gift life could have blessed me with. When I turned 30, I came off the pill expecting it to take a few years as I'd been on pill since meeting my man. He is the only man I've slept with and the only man I've ever loved. We were childhood sweethearts, we are both devoted to each other. He is a beautiful, wise, honest, loyal soul and without him I couldn't grow or learn because he's like my teacher; he teaches me patience, and that there are more important things in life than things. He is a very grateful man who does everything for everyone without wanting to be recognised. He really is a true gentleman; he wants credit for nothing. He works day and night to better his business which he started three years ago and has not given up on it, working all hours to put things right. Not only is he hardworking but also an amazing dad who loves his son unconditionally.

I've been with my man seventeen years, not once have I heard him call anyone out; that's the truth, he's so forgiving, he just wants a peaceful life. He does not suffer fools or try to impress anyone and I have so much to thank him for. We are best friends and I count my blessings every minute of every day that we understand and respect each other and, as unreal as it sounds, we never row or fall out, we just forgive. Our son is two years old and has never witnessed us even shout because we don't. My man lets me be free, allows me to be me, and makes me feel like the free spirit I am. With him by my side, I feel alive - nothing could buy the love I feel for him and how complete I feel to have a beautiful child to such a perfect soul. His parents and family are good people, and I've lived with them half of my life. They are so different to my parents, I get peace when I come home, and have lots of fun and banter with my side of the family. I wouldn't change a thing about any of my family because I let them be them, and I will be me. I am happy, free and I love life. I make the most out of whatever situation I find myself in, and I believe we always learn from others. We learn patience, love, strength and that not everyone thinks or acts the same because they are not you, so never try to change a person because they may not choose to understand you, just like you may choose not to understand them. We have to just forgive, move on and focus on ourselves. Even your partner may never do what you expect from them, but they're not you so don't try to rule them; they're a free spirit, with a free mind and don't judge them - let them be them and you be you.

In school I was never brainy and never interested in getting As, Bs and Cs. I always knew I would be ok and I had qualities others didn't, such as people skills and communication. I was friendly, caring and kind. I loved to write poetry and stories, and even though I wasn't the best speller, I had an amazing imagination.

I always felt different, I'd sing in school choirs - solos every time - I loved to sing. At Christmas I'd go carol singing at people's doors. I wasn't a Christian but I'd always thank God for everything every day and go to the church on a Sunday. I always had a belief that life is whatever you make it and without ever reading a bible, have always naturally been a good Samaritan. I love nature, the sky, the stars and people, I've always been one to solve a problem rather than create one, and I've always known what's not good for me. I don't hate anyone; I just forgive them. I always said I should be a nun because I have always done right in my heart, I just do my best. Being a nice person means I am emotional, sensitive and wear my heart on my sleeve, but I have learned that not everyone in life will understand you; equally so, not everyone has to understand you. People will hurt you but only if you let them, and people will learn - it may just take them more time to do so. I love the person I am, the person I was and the person I have become; I am still me, just on a higher level and I wouldn't change a thing. I appreciate, respect and love everything I have, including the people I have around me. To some, I may have nothing, but to me, I have everything I need. Who needs cars, money, and fancy houses when you have love, trust, commitment, truth and beautiful, inspiring people in your life?

I learned many years ago to take the good with the bad, never make a mountain out of a molehill, and to always remember that a feeling is just a feeling; it will always pass, and by dwelling on a bad thought, it will only make everything seem worse. Nothing has to be a problem unless we choose to make it one and life is only what we make it. You cannot go round blaming others for how you are feeling, and you have to remember we all hurt, suffer, feel lost and feel used, but it's up to ourselves to mope or cope. I'm the type of person to have a pound in my purse and spend the whole day being positive about it because shit happens. I had my little boy and lost my driving license for speeding, I am a mobile hair dresser with no car but rather than complaining, I've got on with it. We walk in wind, hail and rain to every job. We take the good with the bad, we don't have much money but we make every day count. I always say ride the wave of life, don't complain when you have nothing because really nothing is everything in a grateful person's eyes. I know a grateful person when I see one, a good person and a needy selfish person, but we are all human and we will learn. A great attitude is key. We don't have to be happy every day, we just have to be grateful and know it is ok not to be ok. I now look back on all the beautiful, wonderful things I have brought to me by asking, believing and working hard for everything I want from life.

I never thought I'd want to model, catwalk or win pageants until the thought came into my head and I then made it happen. I don't believe in luck; I believe in working hard to make happen what you want from life, and be kind to yourself if things don't work out - because at least you have tried it. It all depends on how much you want it. You can sit back and expect everything to fall to you on a plate, but, unless you have dreamed hard, worked hard and put in effort to achieve it, it will not happen. Always make the best out of whatever situation you find yourself in. I'd write down at 11 years old, that I wanted to be a successful hairdresser and work in a top salon. I worked for Voodou; Toni & Guy; Avant Guard; and went on an interview with Vidal Sassoon. I always wanted to do film, drama, dancing, and singing. I worked for Hollyoaks; was in Annie; Oliver; a play about the war, and went for many auditions. I was into dancing and sang solos in every school play, and from day one I have striven for what I want from life and made it happen, such as cars, holidays, clothes, relationships, love, respect, happiness and so on. The law of attraction to me is no secret; it is what it is - simple as. We are all amazing and we all bring events, people and experiences to us through thought. We choose what we want from life - what is so hard about that? If I can wake up with no money in my purse or no money in my bank and bring to me a grateful, happy, pleasant day then that is a great day for me. I've taken myself to London and got promotion, jobs, won crowns, raised money for charities and even did a sky-dive in May 2015.

I do make-up, hair and beauty; I've been in many hair competitions, won hair awards in London, won modelling competitions and been in photo shoots and fashion shows. I've met people from every walk of life, been to fabulous locations and invited to many events. This is not ego talk, just pride, knowing that anything is possible. If it's what you really want, then you will make it happen.

I've learned that what's really important are the simple things in life that money can't buy; and being really grateful is so important. Okay, so money is great; it buys us fancy clothes, so that we look good. I looked great when I worked in the city, was as bright as Avaline from Bread and as trendy as Herbert of Liverpool. I loved buying clothes, paid for all my own driving lessons and passed my test. My beautiful granddad helped me with my first car, and then I wanted a new registration and wouldn't settle for an old car. I suppose I was a bit greedy, and foolish. It's ok to want nice things, but if you're not truly grateful and thankful for them, then it's pointless. I have to say there is no better feeling than being independent, paying for all your own holidays and knowing everything you bring into your life has been through hard work; but when you have experienced it, as well as having experienced having nothing, you then have more of an understanding of knowing what it feels like to have nothing. How happy you choose to be after all of the pain, hurt, lessons and life's ups and downs, is what makes you the person you become. We are forever learning and if we aren't learning then we haven't lived.

One of my biggest lessons in life would be how I thought working my arse off to have everything I have ever wanted was going to bring me happiness, but it never really did. What it did, was teach me losing my job, losing my car, having nothing but to then find happiness. It takes strength, time, patience, love, gratitude and just knowing that everything will be ok. Life is not a race; live in the moment, love life and love the person you are. I love the person I am and right now, I have nothing but love, understanding and knowing; like I knew it was the best thing to do when I walked out of my job to spend 18 weeks next to my granddad's hospital bed, because he was more important. I knew everything would be ok, like I know he is OK and all around us every day, in spirit.

I see him, feel him, hear him, and I get signs from him because I believe.

I'd just turned 30 and I remember clearly lying on a white, sandy Jamaican beach, with the sun beaming in my face and not a cloud in the sky - listening to nothing but the sound of the waves. I felt so relaxed and free, reflecting on life and feeling proud of how far I'd come and how the holidays, and meeting lovely people had come through working, travelling and being the outgoing, hard-working person I am. For as far back as I can remember, I always knew that your own happiness is through choice. I remember being 18 and getting my first wage packet, and knowing that if I didn't book my first holiday that I wouldn't get one if I didn't make it happen myself. I booked my first ever holiday with my boyfriend at 18 and went back six months later because I loved it so much, we have away every year since. Everything I've experienced, had or achieved in my life, I've gone out and made happen because I believed in myself and that I could do it, and so I did.

I've always had a good understanding of life and people, and I've always believed that what you give out you get back. Karma works in mysterious ways; give out good, you get good. Give out bad, you get bad. So, no matter what, always do good.

I believe I am naturally a good person, but I've met people, many people, who I've really admired and looked up to, yet they have so much self-doubt. If only they could see in themselves what I could see, like my mum who has brought up four children and puts us all before herself, her own wants and needs; she really is such a beautiful person, inside and out. As much as I have lots of great qualities, I'd never be half the woman she is; only she chooses to pick out her faults and imperfections. What I don't like to do is criticise myself, because I believe enough people in life will do that for you. One thing that I've learned is that people will go around being unkind to you, no matter what, because they are unhappy with themselves, or they wouldn't go around making other people feel bad or blaming others for how they feel. Also, I believe that if you love yourself enough, you really won't take interest in other people being critical towards you, because you know your own worth and people can be very draining, but only if you let them drain you.

I always say that if you have your own mind, be your own kind of beautiful and let others be theirs without judging. I've learned that always being positive and clearing your mind from any trash is always best. I felt so enlightened with positive thinking and a positive mindset, that I thought I'd mastered it all, but I clearly didn't and I still slip. I do become instantly aware of my behaviour and know if I'm being hard on myself. I used to think that positive thinking brought anything and everything to you, but I know now that bad things can still happen. Things can go wrong, however, it's all about how you respond, react, feel and allow others to treat you or affect you. Life is one big lesson and, at 33, I'm still learning.

I used to kid myself that I was psychic in a way that I could read minds, but I now believe I just feel energies. I only have to walk in a room and I instantly feel if someone is hurting, feeling bitter, angry, jealous, envious, sad, happy or positive and whether they are having a good or a bad day. Their body language, how they respond, how they talk and the words they use say it all. Energy for me is something I pick up on and, yes, I believe I have a gift, but I didn't always know I had it. I just thought it was normal to be kind and caring, to help others, say nice things, see good in others, treat everyone fairly and be happy for people getting on in life or doing well. As I got older, and had my son, I realised we live in a world full of hate, drama, negativity, envy, bitchiness, violence and selfishness. I feel that getting hurt by others only made me stronger and made me realise I never want to be like some of the people I've been around or been hurt by. They have only made me see how many good qualities I do really have that others haven't got.

I like to see the good in everyone, to believe we are all born pure and innocent, and that we just pick up bad habits, addictions or other issues along the way.

Society is one big rat race with people trying to outdo each other and have better things. Most people seem to think that money is power and it is certainly not, unless it is earned, respected and used to help others or help oneself in a way that is not coming from greed or selfishness. No selfish act is big or impressive. I always say you should be true to who you are and never lie to yourself, love yourself from deep within, love all your imperfections, don't try to impress anyone but yourself, and always be real. If other people seem to be doing well and you feel that you're not, in some way, then be happy for them and know that we are all just born to learn. So if you give good then good will always come back, and if you believe in yourself then you don't need anyone else to believe in you, because it's your life, your lessons and your journey, not theirs.

Of course there have been times when I've thought I was a bit odd, such as when all of my friends would be partying at the weekend and I'd be sitting in, looking at four walls, and just feeling grateful to be alive. I met my man when I was young, which meant partying, clubbing, impressing others was never for me. I was never a 'sheep', so to put it, following the crowd and other people's rules, and I always had my own mind. I never just agreed with others I have no time to be fake as I just simply don't agree with it. I have lost friends through not agreeing with what they say, I have distanced myself from drama and shit-talk all my life. I can't be around bullshit and if people don't understand that then they don't deserve me.

I am one of the most caring, kind, hardworking, loyal people, and because I'm a very independent person, I don't like people fussing over me - I like to just do things myself. I say, 'If you want something doing, then do it yourself' don't expect from others or you will never get anything done'. For as far back as I can remember I've always lived with gratitude and respect for both myself and others. I wasn't the smart one in school; if anything, I wasn't interested in school. I used to write poetry in maths lessons and never paid a blind bit of notice to the teachers. If anything in life, I've taught myself everything I need to know and it's been my mum who has taught me the most valuable lessons, that love and kindness cost nothing but get you through anything in life. If you can love, then you can live without anything but love.

I've spent most of my life being a good person, living, learning, forgiving and seeing the good in life. I am very open, outspoken real and honest. Happiness doesn't mean you have everything you want, it means you are happy and grateful with everything you've got, no matter how little it is. Knowing you can have, be or achieve anything you want doesn't mean you are going to be happy when you get it. I'd say it's about enjoying every second of every day, even through the hard times; because if you can get through the hardest times with a grateful heart, then you can get through anything. Ok, life is meant to be joyful and abundant but it doesn't mean we don't have hard times, up and downs, highs and lows. Without them, we would never learn anything, because getting through the hard parts makes us stronger, wiser and more grateful than ever. My son has taught me what real love is and what really matters, what's important and what's not. I've done many things in my life to make me proud but nothing more proud than being a mummy to the most beautiful boy I have ever set eyes on, he's everyone I've ever loved and cared for, all rolled into one. I don't teach him anything, I just watch him grow and learn, and I don't take a second of him for granted, I never have. He is my life, my everything and the reason I'm strong enough to write my first book.

I know what it feels like to have no car, no job and no money, to feel lonely, lost and like I'm on my own. Sometimes you can be in a room full of people and still feel like the whole world is against you, that no one really cares. I also know how it feels to feel love, joy, happiness and that everything is going smooth and perfect. I like to turn a bad into a good, I have to see the sunny side of life. I believe that feeling sorry for yourself will solve nothing and that you aren't a victim unless you choose to be one. I believe that no matter what is going on around you, you can either make a situation worse or choose to make it better by walking away or not thinking about it, dwelling and focus on the good stuff, not the bad. So, ignore the bad and the good will soon come; don't think second best. "Be number one, spread some love, don't give to receive, strive to be happy and live to believe" – Jessie J.

Chapter 6 - Becoming Mum

I've always believed that you choose your own thoughts and that if you think the worst then the worst will happen, because that is what you are choosing to believe. For example, you can't get rid of baby weight once you've had a baby, or girls are criers, or your baby should sleep at this time, or your boyfriend should be doing this or that. Believe me, it's your life, no one else's and you need to do what makes you, not other people, happy. I loved every second of my pregnancy because I chose to love every second of it. I had no sickness, no tiredness, no heartburn, no pains and no cravings; I ate what I wanted and when I wanted. I went 10 days over and loved every second, was started off, was 10cm dilated with no pain. I was calm, even though I knew my placenta was coming first and that it was so dangerous. I was rushed in for a section and was in hospital with my baby for a whole week.

It was the best experience of my life. Meeting my son was the best feeling ever, bonding with him in the hospital, seeing my man supporting and looking after us. All the staff in the hospital were amazing, I have so much to thank them for, it was the most overwhelming feeling ever bringing my baby into this world, meeting his beautiful little face for the first time. There is no love like it and no emotions like it. I will count my blessings for the rest of my life. Life really is a miracle and we are all blessed, some of us just choose to believe that we are not blessed, because of the negative thoughts which can get in the way we don't always realise the beauty of what life has to offer in so many ways. Since becoming a mum I'm most certainly a better person. I don't claim to be perfect and I don't choose to lie to myself. Everything I say out loud or write down is truth, I would never lie to myself because I really believe that every thought and action, and the way you behave or treat others comes right back around to you, whether it's good or bad. Life is one big lesson, your higher self will always guide you and tell you if something doesn't feel right, then you will make a choice and if it's the wrong choice you will know. You're the master of your own life, you create your own life by every thought you choose to think. What you put in is what you'll get out of life; it's simple. If you don't want drama then walk away from it, don't create it, don't talk bad about others and let others live how they wish to live; focus on your own life. When you focus on yourself, you will become a lot happier, as other people's problems can be draining which can distract you from getting on with your own life. Never blame other people for how you are feeling because if you allow them to affect how you feel then you only have yourself to blame. I understand it hurts when others treat you wrongly, but we cannot let others bring us down, they have to help themselves and you have to help yourself.

Chapter 7 - My Life Journey

I've done a skydive and it was the most amazing feeling ever. I felt so thankful for the whole experience and it was something I'd always wanted to do. I met some cool characters that day; we had a great time. A lovely couple from Liverpool dropped me off, we talked about how amazing the whole day was, how cool the 'Black Knights' team was in taking us up in the plane and dropping us out of the sky at 15,000 feet. I watched the video footage and cried, I loved it so much. I love meeting new people, I find myself meeting strangers in coffee shops and having deep conversations about life - I just enjoy good conversations. I do believe the more open you are, then the more you attract open conversations, and it somehow seems like it's meant to be. It's as though these people sit right next to you for a reason and it's so clear that they were sent - it's so beautiful. I love life and love people. Not everyone will understand you, but as long as you understand yourself then that's great.

I feel that, with my awareness growing and since having my little boy, things don't hurt me as much as they once did or would. I don't have time for ego driven people who keep telling everyone how spiritual they are, yet seem to think life is a competition, always trying to impress everyone, being rude and unkind to others and claiming they are beautiful, spiritual people; but I see it, rise above it and bless them. I do admit I will always nose on Facebook and write status daily, but I don't like what I see. I am so aware; it's crystal clear to me what path others are on and I've found myself wanting to help a lot of lost people on Facebook, but I have to protect myself. I see a lot of haters and unhappy, bitter, angry people, which is very sad because if truth be known, all I want for others is happiness. I do not judge anyone, in fact, I love individuality but if anyone is unkind to anyone or think they are above the rest, then they have a lot to learn. It's so much easier being nice, and so much more draining hating people. My advice would be to wish them well and focus on your own life rather than getting angry about people. Don't worry why people act and behave the way they do, because there is absolutely nothing you can do to change them. I can't tell you why I have Facebook, because it was out for years and did not interest me until I went self-employed and I wanted to promote my hair dressing. When I joined Facebook, I couldn't even use a laptop and I was all made up with myself learning how to save pictures and post them. I became a bit obsessed with taking pictures of myself, writing statuses and finding nice quotes to share with everyone. I wanted to share the love and was never aware people hated others. I'd always live in my little bubble and genuinely thought everyone was nice because I was nice. Before joining Facebook, I swear I was away with the fairies, and was even on it for a long while before I noticed things like 'aimed statuses' and so-called friends clicking 'like' on pictures of everyone but never mine. If I'm being honest, I got a bit paranoid wondering why my so called friends were really going out of the way to treat me as though I was invisible. I went from never being bothered about what anyone thinks, to questioning why I was so nice to all those people on

Facebook and they were never nice back. That is when I realised how vulnerable I was. When I'd comment, 'You look lovely,' the person would answer another, but blank me. I look back now and think, 'Oh my God, why did I let petty things like that bother me?' but we live and we learn. It was never about being liked, I just couldn't get my head around why people could be so rude. My mum would say to me, 'Dan, where do you find the time to notice these things?' and I really didn't know. I guess I was a Facebook freak.

I really don't know why, because it's laughable, looking back. I don't use Twitter, never have, I don't use Instagram or any other social network. I don't follow celebs, never have, and I can't remember the last time I bought a magazine. I think I was 19, that was 14 years ago, so I don't know who's who, and I don't care. Why I was once bothered by Facebook I'll never know, but, hand on heart, I love a little nose, but it can bore me, especially when you see people's true colours. You do people's hair and they will be calling someone, being all nice to you. I've often had people delete me off Facebook, even groups of girls removed me and then the same group of girls tried to add me; it's bizarre. I've had people communicate with me largely when they want something from me then blank me when it suits them. None of these matter and I do not care, but it has taught me to trust no one but myself. It has taught me to never be affected by Facebook ever again and to come off it if it ever it makes me feel angry, hurt or upset by such pettiness. I will never stop being nice just because others aren't as nice as I am. I've learned that not everyone is going to like me, not everyone is going to understand me, and not everyone is going to be happy for me. Of course we all want to be liked and my greatest lesson in life has been realising that not everyone thinks or looks at life the way I do. A lot of people claim they are spiritual but are certainly too ego driven.

Let's move on from all this negative talk, it's pointless and a waste of thought and energy. Remember we can never move forward in life with negative thoughts. Thinking negatively solves nothing and changes nothing; let it go and grow. My greatest joys in life have been when I have had low points and had to ask my angels for signs; when I have felt that I have really needed to pray and I have felt real energies coming over me and shifting weight, like me losing my license for speeding and having no car. I have had to walk in wind, hail and rain with my little boy to make money but that wasn't a low point, it's been a lesson. We walk so much that I get a lot of thinking time; I find pleasure from a butterfly landing on my hand or seeing two birds, or looking in the sky and convincing myself that the brightest star was following me home. I've seen nature blossom, leaves changing colour, snow turn to ice, and rainbows breaking through dark clouds. I love nature; I love the beauty of life and I'd rather gaze at the sunset on holiday than watch the entertainment. Nature speaks in high volumes, and silence for me says more than words. We can create wonders through energy and everyone, if you tune into the good vibration, then life would be so much more pleasant. Life cannot reward you if you can't be grateful for such simple things, and when you crave money and fame, then you're heading down a very lonely path. I love holidays with my boys (my son and my man), I love my family and love seeing other people happy and getting on in life. I love having conversations with interesting people that go on for hours - I can't seem to pull away from such people, because the conversations are very surreal. We learn from others and help them while they help us. I love healing myself as I know what my own body needs. I know when I need time out, rest or a shit-load of goodness in me. I enjoy different types of good in fact; I love food, I love watching a good film, I love a good cry, I love being sensitive and emotional, and I have a massive heart; it's who I am. I don't regret a second of being overly nice to people, because it's who I am and I couldn't live with myself or sleep at night if I was to know that I'd said or done something to hurt anyone. I always pray and count my blessings, always ask for my angels to show me the way and that if I have ever hurt or been unkind to anyone or myself, for them to forgive me and show me how to be a better, more understanding me. If I am learning every day, then I am growing - I pray for others too.

I could not live being ungrateful, it would have no meaning and it would make me feel miserable. Not a day goes by that I don't count my blessings and I certainly have more good days than bad days, because when I choose to be hard on myself or let others affect me, then I can't blame anyone but myself. People may moan about the rain; I'd rather dance in it. I love musicals, I love Disney films, I'm convinced I've been here before a million times (I believe in reincarnation) and that this may be my last life. It's as though I know I am a real earth angel. I believe I was born to help others and to also help myself of course, because I am not perfect but a touch closer every day to gaining my real angel wings - I want to live forever though. I love my dear family, my best friend and son so much that everyday excites me. Every day I feel blessed.

I have goals, dreams and desires and I want to take my son to Lapland. He is 2½ years old and he has already been to Disneyland, Puerto Rico, Turkey and Fuerteventura. I don't know who loved Disney more, me or him, but it was magical. It was Christmastime and all the trees were lit up - I still sing 'When You Wish Upon A Star' to him now, every day. The Disney Parades were amazing; we sang, we danced, it snowed and it was one of the best Christmas gifts I'd ever bought myself and my little family. Holidays were always about me and Rob, but I could not imagine going away now without our little man; he's as good as gold. My dream is to get us to Lapland to meet Santa in the North Pole. When I have a dream I turn it into a reality, it's something I am good at and it's getting what I deserve and desire from life.

My dream is to write more books, help others as much as I can and help them achieve their goals by believing in themselves even when things don't turn out; because with patience, time, consistency and the right attitude, good will always come. My goals for 2015 were to write my book, 'I Believe In Me!,' let go of anything that does not serve me, spend less time on Facebook, have more productive time, get more done, live in the moment, get a summer holiday, get to Lapland at Christmas, eat healthily, drink water, add more fruit and vegetables to my diet and enjoy every precious moment with my son, partner and family. I like to have goals but they are not important to me, so when they happen it's a bonus and when they don't I just wait patiently until they do, because in the end what's meant to be comes to me at all the right times for all the right reasons.

I feel the whole 33 years of my life has been one big lesson and every experience has moulded me into the person I am today. I can look back and I can admit I once thought I knew it all, but I was just learning. I look at how wise I am now and how much I thought I knew compared to how much I know now - I still have a lot left to learn. Right now, though, I am in a good place, happy and I have nothing to prove to anyone. The things that once bothered me now don't, and I once thought I was always right, but I can now see that I am not. I accept that I am only as happy as I choose to be and by allowing others to distract from my journey, I am only slowing down all the good from coming and letting myself down. Right now I am stronger, wiser and more enlightened than I've ever been, but ten years ago I thought I knew it all and was different from everyone else. Now I know it just is what it is and we learn from each other - every human teaches us something different. They say not to look back and to live in the moment, but I love looking back and I would not change a single thing. I have so much to thank my parents for - I carry all the love I experienced as a child through to my child.

I feel blessed that I was once insecure and had a lot of self-doubt, or I would never have become who I am today. If I had been totally confident, then I would have never known or experienced all the growth. If I didn't know what it was like to have nothing, then I would never have become the grateful person I am. I think life pays you back at all the right times for all the right reasons and it's all down to the attitude, behaviour and life choices you choose to make. One thing I have made is some great life choices and I wouldn't change a thing. I would say to anyone who has had a bad past thought, or made some bad mistakes to let it go, move on, start a new day. It doesn't matter how old you are; it's never too late to change, to make changes or to be a better you. Stop beating yourself up, stop being critical and stop blaming everyone but yourself. Life is what you make it, so let go of all bad feelings and keep all the good feelings coming in. Anyone can be happy, it all starts with you. This doesn't mean to say you should ignore the sad, bad feelings - just let them be, go through it, learn and be kind to yourself. There's no such thing as 'can't' when you can. No-one is in charge of your life but you so stop comparing yourself to how others live, and live how you wish to live. If you have a bill to pay and you feel like having a treat, and then go have the treat, the bill money will appear, it always does. My point is, life is how you want to structure it to be, and how you live your life is down to your choices. Every choice has an outcome as a result of what you take action on. You need to know your worth and stand up for what you believe in. Be proud of who you are and don't let anybody tell you how you should be or how you should live; no one has the right to meddle, simply because it's YOUR life.

It would be great to be young again, without a care in the world, but you can't turn back time. You can however, enjoy the 'now' and every moment. There's no point in dwelling on what you should or shouldn't have done, because it's done and it's been a lesson to learn from. From that lesson, whatever bad experience it may have been, I turn it into a positive by not putting myself in the same situation again, and maybe handle it differently compared to how I may have, to ensure a better outcome. As time goes on, we learn from each and every experience. I learned to love myself and accept all my flaws. I learned to just simply live and be, because life is too short. I do believe you are only as beautiful as you choose to become in all areas.

I love childhood memories; I feel they mould us into who we are, I was very blessed to be loved by my parents and all I remember are happy times because my mum made sure of that. I remember nothing but music, musicals, walks to parks, picnics, always being out and about; my mum never liked sitting in. She had four kids, and she dressed us all in the same colour and called her four children names beginning with the letter D: Danielle, Danica, Dale and Dean. She hand-knitted us clothes and braided our hair for school with matching ribbons. She always had us smart and clean, always in the best gear; I really don't know how she did it. I was always colourful and stood out - everyone says to me now, 'Dan, your mum had fab kids.' No one can say a bad word about my mum, she's beautiful inside and out. When I close my eyes, I have memories of all the love my mum had for her children and everyone around her - nothing but love, time and patience. It was never about her but always her kids. I will never be half the woman she is and I was greedy and self-obsessed before I had my son Dexter, I just wasn't aware of it. Whereas my mum went without, I lived before I had my son, yet my mum has put everyone before herself. I know what it's like to have money, cars and holidays; my mum knew no different, but what I know now is that nothing is worth more than the love my mum has left with me, because I can carry that onto my children. In my eyes love is everything, just some people are too greedy and self-obsessed to even know that nothing else matters except how you love yourself and respect others.

Forgiveness is the key and love is everything; if you can't love, then please don't hate. I remember the bedding I had as a kid, Snatch the Dog with bean bags and matching curtains. I remember our rooms were always decorated with whatever we loved at the time. I loved Forever Friends and had all its collection; Care Bears was another one. I loved having a room full of imagination, my mum's house was always full of love and she would let all my friends around, wanting to make them all chips and chicken drumsticks. When it was raining outside, she would let us all run in to dry off. A home was to be lived in and a messy house was just how we liked it. My mum would sit for hours knitting, making us clothes and different pram covers with material. She would let me sing all over her house and bring my friends in the back garden to make up dance routines, because we thought we were going to make it as a girl band. Ha ha! I had dream boxes under my bunk beds, full of goals and things I wanted to achieve. There were pictures of places I wanted to visit and holidays I'd like to go on. Jobs I wanted and poetry I'd write, love letters from Robert, Valentine's cards, songs I'd written, letters from friends - I still have them all now. I've always come in, got snug and written notes and diaries since I was about 10 years old. I miss living with my mum, I miss cleaning my room and moving all my sister's stuff around, I miss Mums house, I miss wearing my sister's clothes and her saying, 'hey that's mine.' I miss my brothers telling me I looked like a mess in my orange dungarees and my mum saying she wished we didn't all hate each other, "as if we did hate each other." Family means everything to me, no matter what; memories are forever floating in my thoughts. I have some amazing childhood memories and no greater feeling than love and gratitude for all I was blessed with as a child; the list goes on. I would give my family anything and if I could wish for anything for them, it would be peace, contentment, shelter, warmth, love and respect for each other. All I ask is that they are happy and grateful because I am so grateful to each and every one of them. I could write a book just about my family but I won't and never will.

I am me; I am my own person, spirit and soul. I have my own mind, I make my own choices. I am independent, hardworking and am pretty much in my own little bubble. I always say, 'Let me be me and you be you'. I don't tend to listen to others, I'd much rather listen to my inner self and do what feels right rather than what others advise me to do. I walk my own path and live by my own rules; that is just my way. I don't involve myself in anyone's problems or dramas but that doesn't mean I don't care, it just means I care about myself too much to be weighed down by any negativity or pointless drama. I feel blessed that I am great with my hands, that I can do any type of haircut, style, colour or creation, and that I have clients who love me and my son so much that they even allow me to bring him to work.

My clients read and play with Dexter and I get paid for something I love. I'm passionate about it. I've been hair dressing for 17 years and I don't think I've had a day without my scissors in my hand; every day is an adventure for me. I like to step out of my comfort zone; what mobile hairdresser has no car and walks in the wind, hail and rain to every job, taking her little boy with her? We sing in the rain, have play time, lunch and breaks in between jobs. We don't complain, why would we? We have each other and I have legs; not once has working been a problem and being a mummy is the best 24/7, job I've ever had. I love being a mummy. The singing, hairdressing mum who is now a beauty queen! I call myself a real princess and my son is my prince. I have been called many things but never an author, but the best title I give myself is the word 'Me', because I love being me. I love people, love how we are all different, all imperfect and all learning. Life is too short in my eyes and if others hurt us, we must forgive every day. One thing about me is that I always make an effort with people, always, as you never know what they could be going through or how they are feeling.

I want to grow old with no grudges; I don't want to carry anger, bitterness, hate, envy or guilt with me. That is why every day I let go and move on; every day is a new day. I will not let anything or anyone get me down, no matter what energy they carry. If I am not living life in my happy little bubble then I am doing something wrong in my eyes; everything for me has to be about good flow, good energy, good feeling and good vibration. Every second of every day has to be about positive thought, action and behaviour and if I'm not consistent in all I do, then I feel out of sync. I instantly know when I'm dwelling on something because my mood shifts and my energy is so low. It's like my body knows it's no good for me to feel down or to be hard on myself.

To all my family, I want to thank you for all my memories, all the hard times we have been through, all the precious moments we have shared. The people we have lost and the tears we have cried, through good times and bad times. Family is where the heart is, nothing else matters but to see the people you love are ok, because when you know your family is hurting then you are too and there is absolutely nothing you can do about it; especially when you have a different perspective of life and understanding but they don't. They don't see what you see or feel what you feel, they don't believe what you believe in, but that does not mean you have to give up on them even if they feel like giving up on themselves. I feel very blessed to have a good outlook on life and through some very hard times when I could have given up, I chose not to and I've got through it because I've had to be strong, otherwise I wouldn't be where I am today. I could list a million things I could complain about every day, and a million other things to be grateful for. My little boy keeps me going, I've never known love like it. He is my everything and not once have I ever found him hard work. He's my miracle, my life saver and the reason I get up every morning.

Chapter 8 - Letting Go

For some reason I feel like my book needs to be written and include everything that I need to let go of, just so that I can move on. I need to let go of any anger or tension I am carrying with me in order to let go and start a new chapter of my life; I feel that until this book is complete, then I won't be. I feel it's my calling, my time, and if I don't do it now then I will never find the time. I believe that then won't be the right time but now is. I feel a lot of people, in fact most, don't feel like they are good enough, that's why they spend more time unhappy, thinking they are victims and that life has got it in for them when really they have it in for themselves. They just blame anyone they can to make themselves feel better. I feel if we ventured into ourselves more, then we would understand that life is what you make of it. I want to move on from all the nonsense in life and away from all the people that create it; I just want to simply live. I know how it feels to be really hard on myself and never want anyone to dwell on a bad feeling and feel as low as low really feels. We are all human and I think you have to experience feeling very low and alone to understand how another person may be feeling, but please remember it is ok and you are ok. You could lose everything and then gain from it, you just have to stay strong and believe.

When you're a mum you don't get time to think straight, but I've written this book because I believed I could, so I did. You can succeed too, in whatever you wish to achieve; you must never give up on something that you strongly believe in. I could put pen to paper and write forever because I am a passionate person and very passionate about life. I don't claim to be right or wrong and not everyone will agree with me or believe in what I believe in, but I believe in myself so much and it feels good. When I feel good, it's great, that is why I am always thankful for good feelings, and then life brings to me more of the good stuff which makes me even more thankful, but when I am down, it sucks. That's why I don't want anyone to choose negative, dwelling thoughts that aren't good for you.

I always find when you give time, love, understanding and support to others, life has a way of paying you back in so many ways when you least expect it. I've found that thoughts that drain you really don't serve you, and focusing on your own growth is not selfish. It's very important because when you dwell, worry, stress and care about what others think of you, it affects your whole body. You are in charge of yourself and you cannot blame anything or anyone else for the way you are feeling; even posture, lack of exercise, too much of anything like foods, thoughts, actions or behaviour all brings to you the life you live and that's good or bad – your choice. It's as simple as A-B-C, we just go around the world to realise it just is what it is and it is all down to you. Simply be happy, do well, be good, give good and feel good.

All I ask for at the moment is that my family know how much I love and care for them, how by them being just them and loving me for just being me, has taught me so much in life. It has made me the loving person I am today. I hope to write more books, help more people, help women and mums to realise their worth. I ask for protection, happiness, health, wealth and abundance but only what I deserve. I ask for forgiveness for any hurt I may have caused to anyone, and I ask to be guided; to show me if I need guidance, to help me be a better me, day by day. I ask for help to put others first before my own selfish needs and wants when need be, but to still experience the beauty and joy from life. I ask for joy, freedom, a nice new chapter and new beginnings for my son and my partner. I ask that my family are happy, content, comfortable and loved.

I think it's time for me to experience new beginnings, whether it be a new home, travel, car or book. I don't know what, but I do know it's time for change. I can feel a change coming and it's all mindset, higher frequency and simply that. I feel we would all love to be loved, feel more appreciated, more thanked for the way we love and respect others, but I have also learned that not everyone knows how to show love or how to please another person in how they like to be pleased. So the best thing to do is to love yourself so much that you no longer get angry or question why people aren't pleasing you because you are too busy pleasing yourself. It is not selfish to take care of yourself, it is necessary because another person cannot do it for you. They cannot please you so don't expect them to.

I could sit here and think, 'I don't have this or that and others have more than me or get more given to them than I do,' but one thing I know is that they will never be me and all the money in the world can't buy a good heart; when you are at peace then you have everything money can't buy.

Chapter 9 - Sky Dive

It had been something I'd always wanted to do so I rang up, paid the £50 deposit and that was that. It was such an amazing feeling from start to finish. I filled out a few forms, had a little safety induction, put the suit on and up we went in the plane - such a buzz! I can't understand why I wasn't nervous, I just knew I had to live in the moment and enjoy ever second.

The cameraman called us the A team because everything went perfectly from the word go, jumping out of a plane at 15,000 feet, strapped to such a fantastic instructor who got me to ground safely. Floating with my feet on top of the world, spinning around, and hanging from a parachute looking at blue skies, breathing in life and feeling blessed. It was truly amazing. I love how we dropped out the air when we were flying in the sky and the cameraman was right in front of me. I couldn't catch my breath, but was beaming with thankfulness that I was safe and felt like I was flying without wings. I loved it so much.

Thanks to all at Black Knights Parachute who made that day possible for me.

I've done some amazing things in my life but for me it's not things that are important, it's the memories I have made and the people I have met along the way. I could list the places I've been and the things I have done, but what matters to me is who I am and how far I have come, that everything I have achieved or experienced has come from me and my belief. Having self-worth to know that I can have, do and be anything if I really want it and the word 'can't' has never entered my mind, let alone 'what' 'ifs' and 'buts'. I like to just make it happen.

Chapter 10 - Loving

You must learn to love yourself no matter who you are. Loving yourself heals everything and when you learn to love everything about yourself, then you can help others. Loving yourself means accepting who you are, forgiving yourself, letting go, not dwelling and not being hard on yourself. Having a good understanding, means you can forgive other people even when they choose to be unkind.

If you can sit in a room with someone who is being nothing but critical towards you and not react or be unkind to them, it just shows how much you understand that they are being unkind and you're not. To be as bad as the way they are treating you would only make you as bad as them, but to understand means you're more aware, and have more understanding. Anyone being unkind normally has a build-up of anger, envy, hate and bitterness. This doesn't make them bad people, it just means they do not love themselves enough, choosing to beat themselves up by being hard on themselves and unkind to others.

We can all help ourselves, it doesn't matter how old you are, what shape, size, height, weight or upbringing. We can choose to be a better person every day. By being a better person, it means we can make the world a better place. I'd say start by focusing on all the good in life. If there's anything that makes you feel bad, don't think about it; it's not worth a thought. Acknowledge it in a way of trying to understand it and what lesson it has brought to you, in order to grow and become a better person.

An innocent child doesn't think about anything bad until he or she picks up bad habits from adults with bad behaviour. Picture yourself as a newborn, an innocent little blessing that knows no bad and breathes in all good. A child doesn't know what money, worry, or stress is. This is all nonsense that we choose to believe and are made to focus on. Who said we have to focus on all the bad stuff? I believe that if we don't think about what's weighing us down then it will gradually disappear, because we have created it in the first place with the thoughts we choose to think. I believe no matter how low you feel or how much we think we can't get out of a black hole, we can, and we just need to change our mindset. If you don't believe you can, then you never will, but if you choose to help yourself and not blame others, then life can be joyful not hateful and you can start being grateful not unhappy.

Look in the mirror and change yourself. If you want to change, start with tiny steps and learn to crawl again, then walk and then fly. I believe each and every one of us is unique, I see good in everyone and see in everyone what they cannot see in themselves. I've always been aware, always been a natural healer and always been able to help myself. I've been low, hurt, used and taken for granted and I've felt pain, hard pain. I have been lost, I fall down but get myself up every time, coming back stronger than ever, and I believe we really do only have ourselves, because after all it's me, myself and I that gets me though my hardest times.

I love being me, love the person I am and love life's experiences because without hard times we would never learn to be strong. If we don't have things taken away from us we would never appreciate what we do have. I've learned to take the good with the bad and to know that life hits us all hard at some point but pain, hurt and suffering doesn't last forever. Maybe it lasts longer for some or less for others, but a feeling is just a feeling that will always pass if you don't dwell on it - it's never good to dwell.

I'd say forgive, learn from it, move on and never hurt the people you love, because you choose to think that they don't care, or that they don't love you or that they don't do enough for you. Try to realise we are all human, the person who you're being hard on is not you and they don't think like you so never expect them to. They are their own person, like you are your own person. If you try to understand them rather than pick out all of their faults, and maybe take a look at your own behaviour before you call others then life would be a lot simpler. Life does not have to be hard but we choose to make it that way.

See the good in all you do and life will see the good in you; try to bring out the best in everyone around you even if they aren't so nice to you because they need it more than you. We all need kindness, it costs nothing. Love makes everything better, forgiveness heals others, letting go and not dwelling solves problems that could occur if you choose to dwell on a thought. Life is short and precious, so never envy anyone because we are all trying to do our best.

Remember, people who seem to have it all really don't necessary. If they cannot be grateful, then they will never be happy. Happiness is not wealth, it's truth. Honestly, it's finding yourself and accepting who you are, knowing that anything is possible if you put your mind to it. We really can have or be anything we want and when we know that, then that is happiness because it's belief. I say be grateful for everything and expect nothing because one day you can have it all and if you aren't grateful for it, it will or can be taken away from you.

If you can be happy with nothing but love, then that is true happiness. I think it's good to have a goal, a plan and to know what you want because if you don't know what you want it's hard to achieve your goals. I look back on my life and I've had a notepad, a diary and 'to-do' lists since I was at least ten years old. Everything I experienced growing up, like holidays, jobs, cars and hobbies have all been through having a thought, writing it down and then making it happen. My life has always been so busy with jobs, hobbies and getting things done that I've never really had time to read. Reading never interested me, then, since my granddad passed away after I read 'The Gift', I now read a lot of self-help books and I believe the books come to me to remind me of what I already know. I now enjoy reading.

Every time I read a book, I'd think I could write a better book myself because I already have all this knowledge. A lot of people seem really shocked about how positive thinking can change them for the better but for me it's natural to think that way. I look at it as life is hard enough so make the best out of what you've got. I see life only has to be a problem if you choose to make it one. I don't think some people have it harder than others, but they choose to make it harder by dwelling on all that's going wrong rather than trying to make it right. Life is meant to be beautiful in all areas so choose to see the good not the bad. It sounds simple because it is; we just choose to think it's not. I dream a dream, try my best to make it a reality and most things I want I get because I believe I can, so I do. I have fabulous experiences, I meet lovely people and I get to do things that I enjoy. I've never wanted a lot of money because I have always thought it was selfish to be greedy, but I've learned that when you're a grateful person you can live with a lot of money, or with very little money. We need enough to get by and anything else is a bonus, a luxury or something we should always be grateful for. If you can't be grateful or be thankful for what you already have, then how can you expect or deserve anything better? Never take life for granted if you want to be happy.

You don't have to be famous, rich or successful to write a book; you just have to be honest enough to write down how you feel and what real-life experience you have been through. I live by the truth; I don't live to impress others. I live to make the world a better place and to make sure everyone around me is happy. If I've left a person with a smile on their face feeling good about themselves, then I've done my bit in the world. Self-worth is a key to happiness. If you don't love yourself and respect yourself, how can you expect anyone else to?

One day I looked in the mirror and I just said to myself, 'I'm going to love all my scars, freckles and other things I didn't like,' and, from that day on, I've never looked back. I started to recognise the voice in my head and if I had a bad thought or feeling, I'd just acknowledge it, walk away from it and not think about it any longer.

I now don't think of anything negative and when I do, I'm instantly aware that it doesn't feel right. I've programmed my mind to think only happy thoughts and I can honestly say if I feel low, down or hurt then I only have myself to blame for allowing a person with a problem to make it my problem because really it's not my problem, it's theirs. When you walk in a room and all a person wants to do is moan, complain and see the bad in everything or everyone, it's not my problem, it's theirs. They blame everyone for how they are feeling but never look at their own faults, actions and behaviour.

The thing is I see right through them, they lie to other people; they manipulate and want to be recognised for all they do but never see good in others or what others do for them, they just want all the credit. The problem with most people like that is they forget that the law of attraction - karma, God, spirits, universe, higher self, whatever you wish to call it, - will see it and you only get from life what you put in, simple as.

If you go around putting others down, being envious, greedy etc, then karma will just come and take away from you everything you think you are in control of.

I used to think that God was watching over me as a child, and that the angels were guiding me, and I used to think that the little voice in my head was a little spirit telling me when I did wrong, but I now believe it's my higher self. None of us have the answers but I know life is only what you choose to see and all I see is the good because I choose my life to be spent as pleasantly as it can be. I choose to make life great, not to be distracted by others as I only have one shot so why spoil it being miserable. Do Good; Be Good; Say Good; Feel Good - all is good in my world because of me.

Of all the people I meet in life, all the experiences I've had, nothing compares or will ever compare to the love I feel for my child - no money, no house, no car. No, nothing matters except love, respect for yourself and others, living in the moment and being grateful, not hateful, and enjoying every second of life. A child is a precious, innocent, pure being who takes everything in like a sponge. A child only knows what you teach it or what it chooses to believe, so remember we are all that child and we can all change how we act, think or choose to behave. Life is all about state of mind and a child doesn't see all the bad, so you don't need to either. It's all just nonsense and what humans have decided to let take over the good. Remember there is good in the world and there is beauty all around us always.

We often all feel low, like we have to prove our worth to people. I don't know why though. I think we feel we have to be accepted but to value yourself is a much greater feeling than wanting to be valued by others. I always say if you are in a negative state of mind, it's just a thought and it will pass, don't dwell on the stuff that's bringing you down, but focus on all the good feelings. It's so easy to feel low but choosing to mope and be hard on yourself is much harder work; focus on being happy instead.

So when my granddad passed over, I finished reading my first book called The Gift. The author of the book, whose son had died at a young age, couldn't get her head around why, that if she had a gift then, she didn't know her son was going to die. She did many readings and stopped them, until one day a couple came to her as they too had lost their own child very young and they couldn't understand why either. The thing is none of us know why bad things happen, but all I know is everything happens for a reason and that we have to believe in all that is good because what use is it being hard on yourself?

I always say that when you start to believe and I mean really believe, then you see the real beauty of life and you just know that our loved ones are all around us. So getting back, to this book I read, she was just a down-to-earth woman who had a gift; her gift was that she saw spirits and loved ones. She saw her son in someone else's reading when they came to her. Their child came through, both the children came through and that's when she really believed she had a gift, that everything does happen for a reason. Every book I've read since I took an interest in reading has only reinforced what I already know. I find when I read only things on the lines of law of attraction, positivity and self-help that I understand so well, I believe I could write a book myself. I never thought I'd write a book as I wasn't the best speller in school but I was always passionate about life. I always had a really good understanding about my happiness being my own choice. I believe I've attracted every book, every experience, every person; and the reason I'm writing this book is because I believe that I'm meant to.

I know that life is amazing and beautiful, and we are powerful beyond measure because I've experienced it. Put me in a room with a scientist, a teacher, someone from any other walk of life or even a self-help expert, and I will have just as much knowledge, if not more. I have enough understanding to teach them just as much as they could teach me. I love talk about energies, feelings, love and the law of attraction. I could stand up and talk to the world about it because I believe in myself that much.

Okay, my book is very simple but I don't see why it has to be complicated. I am trying to get people who aren't the best at reading or understanding to try to understand it. My point is to simply love yourself, love life and love other; to love your family and friends, forgive, understand, don't compete, just be your own hero, just like my granddad, my mum and my loved ones. Just know by being you, you make the world a better place; never give up on yourself. If things aren't going smoothly, know that they will in time. Just be patient, don't expect too much from life, just try to improve your behaviour and your outlook, and know that you owe it to yourself to be a better person and to find self-worth. The less you depend on others to tell you how amazing you are, the more you'll find it in yourself. When you truly love yourself and know your worth, then life will show you the way, but start with yourself. Don't try and fix others, but fix yourself and others will follow.

Do whatever makes you happy; believe in whatever you want to believe in. One thing guaranteed in life is death, hurt, pain and suffering, but the beauty of life outweighs all that. If you just believe that everything is ok, then it will be. If you believe it's not, then it won't be.

Sometimes, when we are happy, the people we love and care about are down, and often when we are down the people we love are trying to be happy. We can feel like no one is on our side, but we have to understand we all go through it; it is part of life. We are on our own journey, learning our own lessons and dealing with our own issues and insecurities. Try to bring others up rather pulling them down, no matter how unkind they can be; most of the time it's the only way they know how to be at that moment in time of life, not always realising any better. You cannot allow other people's moods, actions, behaviour and opinions to affect you or how you feel. They have to live their own life, you can't live it for them or take personally what another says or does.

I just want to be a good mum, a good daughter, a good friend, a good listener, a good person and a supportive partner. My purpose is to help others and grow from it myself. I find wherever I go, whoever I meet from whatever walk of life, I tend to have really good understanding of a person, and I find myself wanting to help them, heal them or make them realise their worth. We are all beautiful, powerful and we can all be, have and achieve anything we want. We really do have the power to get what we want from life. The question is: WHAT DO WE WANT? Is it really what we need and will it bring us happiness?

I count my blessings a lot; in fact I count every second of every day. Even when everything seems to be going wrong, I make it right. I really do see the good in everything, I am such a happy, grateful person with a heart of gold, and all I want is for the world to be at peace and everyone to see the beauty of this wonderful world we live in. I have a wonderful mother, a fantastic family, and such loyal in-laws, friends, fiancé and son, who lights up my life every minute of the day.

I want to write more books, live each day like it is my last, and let all my loved ones know that I love them and all their imperfections. I want to forgive every second of every day and let go of what I cannot change. I want to make love like the first time I ever did. I want to simply be grateful for my every breath and just do things that make me happy with or without money.

I believe that the more one complains, then the more one feels drained. How can you expect good to come when all you are choosing to think is negative, unhappy thoughts? The world would be so beautiful if everyone just took actions for their own behaviour. I don't have all the answers and I am not perfect. I am no saint but I do my best and don't judge people for how they act or behave.

I have bad habits, I love food, I love dressing up, I love feeling like a girl, I love having a good time and I love wearing make-up, however, I also love stripping all the fakeness away to just simply be me. It's good to have fun and let your hair down but it's also good to be real and know it is ok to not look your best. As long as you feel good inside, then that's all that matters. It doesn't matter about your height, weight, skin colour, whether you work or don't work, have money or don't have money. Believe in yourself, be your own kind of beautiful, and just watch the beauty of life come right to you.

I'd like to add that the grass is never greener and once you've had a taste of something, it isn't all that. I would say love and approve of who you are and always remember you have qualities that others don't. We are all unique, loved, special and amazing. Never wish to be anyone else, but enjoy being you.

I don't believe there is a right or wrong way to live, we just do what we feel is right. Whatever feels right for us I suppose is good enough. We can't possibly give up every addiction. Some of us love food, partying, socialising, drinking, smoking and abusing our bodies. I'd say 99% out of 100% of us have some form of addiction. We could kid ourselves, saying we are totally detoxified, cleansed and on a high spiritual level where nothing gets to us, but I will be the first to admit that I love food, hardly drink, don't smoke or take drugs. I'd say I abuse my body by eating too much but I'm aware of that.

I believe I am mind and soul, but to get the perfect balance I need to control my diet. I do have a slim figure and I don't have much body fat at all. I walk a lot, I'm happy with my body shape; my weight doesn't go up and down. I am blessed to eat whatever I wish and be a size 8-10, but I put that down to enjoying my food and not thinking about what I eat. As they say, your thoughts create your life and my thoughts are always happy, positive, grateful thoughts so I am too busy enjoying my food to ever think about putting on weight. To be honest, it doesn't enter my head; I just eat. It's only lately that I've started to think I should be eating healthily because there are so much these days about cutting out junk food and detoxifying.

I am starting yoga, meditation and relaxation classes on Sundays and planning to add more fruit and vegetables into my life. I intend to still enjoy my food as it's something I love, but it's more about taking care of my body now, as well as my mind and soul. I eat too many burgers, have too much coffee and too many fizzy drinks but the truth is, it's time to get as much goodness in me as I can.

Life's about living, not being hard on yourself. It's about approving of yourself and loving yourself from deep within, no matter what shape or size you are. I'd say to anyone: if something makes you happy, do it. As long as you aren't bothering or upsetting anyone else, then live life to the maximum. Don't be too hard on yourself, and realise that we can all be, have or do anything we want. Never envy anybody when you are more than capable of making it happen for yourself. Relax, breathe, live and be grateful. Life is simply what you make it and it's not a competition, it's a gift. My goal now is to sell this book, help others and start writing my next book.

I believe in me and I believe I can help other mums to believe in themselves too. I believe I have been a life coach all my life; it's just that I don't get paid for it. I give freely with love and understanding, but I am ready to help the world and speak out my truth. Something as simple as being nice, doing good, being grateful and respecting others can be so hard for some because they don't know how, it comes so naturally for me, people can find me a threat. All I have are good intentions for everyone, but having such an awareness, means I pick up their hate, drama and envy. I try to heal and help them, but it can become draining, so now my guard is up. I have to protect myself. As long as I'm learning every day, enjoying life as much as I can and everything is a pleasure not an effort, then I'm ok. As long as I am humble, grounded, easy-going, respecting others and doing my best, then the best is all I can do. I like to live in the moment and make every second count. I like to feel rich, even with nothing, because if I'm always grateful then I'm always getting on.

I now feel it's time to get my book out there and, that way, people may understand why I live in my own little bubble. If they don't, then that's ok. From this, I am hoping to get everyone interested in my book, so

I can continue to write more books and help others. I believe we are all amazing and even the people who don't know their worth or believe in themselves help me, because they teach me. Unkind people also teach me who I'd never want to be, and people with a lot of money can be rude, including those who look down on others. I would never want to think I am better than others because I am not and never will be. They will learn that having money doesn't buy happiness.

I have just done a cat walk for Jackson Fashion in Liverpool, and we beat the Guinness World Record as 5,000 people took part. The catwalk was amazing and once again I met amazing people just like I did when doing my skydive, at 15,000 feet, raising money for Alder Hey. This year I have done photo shoots with beautiful horses which I have organised myself at a nearby stable in Knowsley, as it's where we always walked in the summer as kids and I always dreamed of riding a horse. My whole life has been about thought, vision and action, that is all I've ever believed in.

'DREAM, BELIEVE, ACHIEVE', but never did I think one day I'd write my own book. When something feels so right and comes right from the heart, you just know it's meant to be. I just felt I ought to put pen to paper and my angels started writing my book for me, thanking me for being a good soul and giving good out to the world.

My little boy starts nursery in January, I turn 34 the day of the Mrs Galaxy Pageant on 4th February, and I think it will be my last beauty competition. It's been an amazing journey being part of fashion shows, catwalks, photo shoots, working with different designers, winning sashes, trophies and titles, raising money for charities and helping others. It has been a massive eye opener however. Just when I thought life was giving up on me I never once gave up on myself, and anything I've ever wanted I've made possible, including writing my book.

I have my book published, and as well as mind and soul, it's now time to take more care of my body with yoga, healthy eating and drinking more water, even though I am blessed with my body shape. Maybe in my next book I can tell you the truth about whether healthy eating works for me.

So I'm hoping for this book to do well helping others to know their worth. I know that anything is possible with the right attitude and behaviour. I have more shoots coming up, more fashion shows and designers to model for, but if I'm honest I can feel my life going in a new direction once my son starts nursery, so I'm just making the most of what life has to offer and enjoying it while it lasts. I am not getting any younger and if life gives me a taste of something then I will always have a go, if it feels right to do so, even if it's not important. I believe everything is sent to try us and everything happens for a reason.

It's always good to say you've had a go, even when you look back and think it wasn't all that. At the end of the day, nothing is more important than you and the people who really matter, your health, your state of mind and how you feel. So if something no longer feels right, then move on and keep moving forward even if that means sitting at home with a cup of tea and a good book.

My idea of happiness is that my son is happy, that I live in the moment appreciating not complaining watching good films, reading, writing and meditating, dreaming. I love building others up and creating happy magical memories, I believe in me and my happiness is my book, my writing, my life that I have created, which I can share to help others create a life they love.

Chapter 11 - After Thought

Since writing my book I have grown so much, every day we are learning. I never thought I'd learn to become more Thick-Skinned but I know I have to protect myself from being hurt so much. When you have a heart as big as mine you have to learn to protect it. I no longer have the strength to take on as much consideration for how others act, behave or choose to treat me. I have to focus on my goals in life and let nothing stop me from achieving what I want to achieve. It's so easy to be distracted by people and their opinions, but the thing is, other people aren't going to save you, you have to save yourself.

Only you can help yourself as no-one understands you like you'd like them to, and you really don't need anyone's approval. I've found even being a positive, happy-go-lucky person, I can have down days and I can be vulnerable and open to people that really did not deserve my time, however, deep down what I see in others is only a reflection of me and what others choose to think or say about me is only their business, not mine.

Often when I think I've got everything worked out, I can meet people and think they are as nice as me, only to learn they really don't have a heart as big as mine, and never will; but I've accepted we are all different and I'm no longer disappointed when people are rude and ignorant as we are all facing battles no one knows about. I really do feel like I can only trust very few people and that only I have the answers to what I want from life. In the past I've had many readings, been to spiritual churches, meditation circles, had angel cards, Reiki healing, massaging and yoga and, to be honest, I find myself feeling disappointed and tend to heal others a lot more than anyone's ever tried to heal me. I do believe I have a gift and I do believe I've had to experience being vulnerable in order to have grown.

Deep down, a lot of people who claim to be so called 'enlightened' have so much to learn; in fact, we all do - in my eyes, we are all born to learn and are forever learning. I have a very strong mind and I grow and grow every day so I'm no longer the person I was when I first wrote this book. I will always be Danielle but every day I'm growing.

I could write every day because I am very passionate about life, people and the person I want to become. For me, it's now all about what I want and right now, it's simplicity, healing myself more and for everyone to have a copy of my book and get something from it, because I believe I really do have something very special to give to the world and I cannot go a day without thinking about how I am going to do that.

I know now that it's time for a change, with new focus and new challenges. It's time to really challenge myself and step into a new career after being a hairdresser for all of my working life. I want to heal, help, guide and motivate others. I want to write and do courses to put me in the direction that I am meant to be heading and not be distracted by all the obstacles standing in my way. I am going to follow my dreams like I always have, but this time I'm aiming higher.

I have just done my last pageant. As Mrs Merseyside Galaxy, I was a beauty queen helping my community and city as much as I could. I wanted to really go out my way to help others so I found myself collecting, and asking others for old clothing. I was really focused on giving clothes, shoes and blankets to charity shops. I couldn't walk past anyone without giving them a blanket or money for chips or a cup of coffee. I helped out in a toy appeal in my community, giving, wrapping and collecting new toys for less fortunate kids. I helped promote businesses such as local dance and drama groups that felt close to my heart. I modelled dresses for designers and was sponsored for Galaxy by Brides' World of Liverpool. I did a Santa dash raising money for cancer and built up relationships with businesses, being involved in charity events, fashion shows, catwalks and promotions.

Galaxy was an amazing experience and so was every other pageant I've been involved with. Being in pageants after having my little boy gave me the chance to do something for myself. Every girl wants to feel like a princess, but I felt more than like a princess; I gave it my all and enjoyed every second of it, gaining more confidence than ever before and learning so much about myself along the way. I juggled work, being a mummy and a hobby I really enjoyed a lot.

I now know that after years of hairdressing I want to change my job and give up everything I enjoy to make me work. My beautiful boy started nursery a few weeks ago and my main concern is his happiness and me building a future for him. Although I am all about living in the moment and money not being important, I strongly believe that I cannot ignore what feels so right to do. I have had my fair share of fun and proved I can have, be and achieve anything, but for me it isn't about that. It's about who I am as a person, not what I can have or have had, as I want others to know that they are enough and that without struggles, we would not learn anything.

I have found in all my life experience that my greatest healer is ME, myself, and that no one or nothing can heal or love me as much as I can myself. I live a very busy lifestyle but always find time, every day, to ground myself. I count my blessings constantly and meditate every night. I always sleep dreaming of love, light, colourful rainbows, angels and white horses. I really do feel at total peace and although life circumstances, situations and people can doubt us, I've also found that staying on a positive vibration is the way forward. While feeling low is ok, it also does not serve you well, so I've found dwelling is pointless and taking on everyone else's problems and insecurities does no good for your mind, body and soul - it leaves your vibrations unbalanced.

I've found I've gone back to when I was a kid, leaving school and getting my first wage packet, who didn't care or feel too much and just felt happy without questioning things like 'Do I have enough money to buy myself that?' I find that when you put everyone else's feelings before your own you then feel you're last because you tell yourself you don't deserve, but you do. We all do, and if we all loved ourselves enough then we could all love, respect and bring out the best in each other.

Self-love is key, and now, if I want to make things happen I will, because I can and I deserve to be happy. That doesn't make me selfish, it just means that I find things that make me happy and make them happen without questioning how; I just do. Don't get me wrong, I don't have a greedy bone in my body and price tags don't interest me. I borrow Peter to pay Paul and count my blessings every day with a pound or a hundred pounds. Without all my struggles I would never have been able to write this book but I now know for certain my purpose is to help guide and motivate others.

I feel that I have been soul searching my whole life. It seems to be that for as far back as I can remember, I've been living my life from a soul level. I always had the awareness that I was born to help others because I'm naturally just aware; I feel people's pain, hurt and sadness, and just want to tell them nothing is as bad as it seems. I often questioned my gift and asked myself was I the loopy one, but no longer. I now embrace it and heal myself every day and grow more, day by day. The hard part for me, though, was learning that good people with massive hearts tend to get hurt the most, but the interesting thing is, that we need to go through all the hurt to realise that pain is beautiful. Struggle takes strength, and strength is an achievement.

All the sweat, tears, falls, highs, lows and breakdowns that seem to be the worst times of your life really aren't, because they've made you wiser, stronger and more determined than ever before. I genuinely, hand on heart, thank and bless everyone, because I have learnt it was my own insecurities that allowed others to hurt me the way I allowed them to. I let myself be affected but I grew from every lesson which makes me so grateful to each person.

I've had many readings and I've been vulnerable enough to believe, for a second, what they say. I've been happier than ever and felt more enlightened than ever before and they have said to me, 'You're really hurting, aren't you?'

I live such a busy life with my little boy, hairdressing and juggling everything, but I always find time to meditate. In fact, I meditate every day and night, no matter how tired I feel - I manage to find time. I walk a lot and I mean literally everywhere. I don't put the thought in my head that it's impossible to meditate because I am a mum, so I balance everything and my boy just seems to support me- in fact, he is my rock. I just walk and he breathes in life and I go into meditation while pushing the pram. I count my blessings every second of the day, so for me I'm meditating when I'm not even aware that I am because I'm consistently grateful; when I'm not, I am instantly aware that I am only upsetting myself. For example, I was pushing my pram to do a haircut last week and I sulked a little that my hands were cold and that my little boy shouldn't have to be pushed in a pram in that weather, however, the fact is that the child is a breath of fresh air and never complains. Let's face it, there's no such thing as 'should' as long as I'm doing my best and he is happy so why beat myself up? I find dwelling solves nothing and to focus on all my blessings only brings more pleasant experiences.

I am now going to a higher level of vibration as the energy from my body and soul is telling me to. I feel that I grow and grow and that although I've spent most of my life believing I'm a good soul, and to always love and respect others, and put others first, I'm now really clear on wanting to put myself first. I have never asked my higher-self, angel guides, and spirits for money because I always believed it was a selfish act, which it's not, despite spending most of my life thinking I can get by with nothing but a grateful heart. However, because I also have desires, dreams and ambitions, I also know I've made it all possible and that anything I put my mind to is possible.

I had a bit of a 'crossroads experience' not long ago, questioning whether I should just settle for how my life is or whether I deserve more. I have a strong relationship, a beautiful family and son who I just don't go a day without counting my blessings for. I love my life but why not have bigger dreams? I feel I could be the most patient, strong, wise, independent, hard-working person to ever walk the earth, but I just have this feeling that we all hurt sometimes, and we all have to not always feel in control in order to learn. I've seen better days but I've seen the bigger picture. I find I learn most lessons on my darkest days, and the beauty of life is that it doesn't have to be all wonderful because we are wonderful people bringing unnecessary pain and suffering to ourselves when it doesn't have to be so painful; we just choose for it to be.

So, for once in my life, it is time to take action, but not because I'm ungrateful. In fact, I couldn't be more grateful, but it's taken me a whole lifetime of lessons. I do not regret one mistake because it has made me who I am today and I am sure I will make more. I don't tend to hurt as much as I once did and I never thought I'd learn to become more thick-skinned, but life does that to you. In fact, I love life more than I ever did and I love and respect others more than I ever have. I have more understanding than ever and I forgive so easily. I'm just wiser, more headstrong and know what I want. I heal myself, help myself, protect myself and believe in myself more than ever before.

If I were to write a letter to myself from my soul's higher self, it would be:

Hello beautiful child.
You have come so far, through all of life's distractions that have made you the strong person you are today. I want to thank you for believing in yourself and discovering that you really can put your mind to anything, even when things, people, situations, circumstances, opinions of others, lack of money, struggles, hard times and people are telling you that you are crazy. Well, you're not. You are amazing and we believe in you so much that we have opened another door for you and want you to walk right into its light. We knew you were born

to help others; you are a natural healer, which is a very beautiful gift from higher forces. We just had to let you gather all the tools and let go of every bit of self-doubt you were holding onto, and we are so happy that you finally have completely let go. Welcome, sweet child, to the freedom you always had. You just had to search for 33 years for it. Welcome to this new light of love, understanding, bliss, peace, joy, healing, guidance, strength and abundant prosperity. I am excited for you as this is what you were born to do and we are so happy that you have found your purpose and taken action. We look forward to your book being published to help so many others and how you have taken action to follow your dreams and we will be right behind you. We have watched you grow, blossom and bloom. Now you are ready to shine your light over those that need guidance, help and direction and we wish you all the happiness and success that you deserve.

Lots of love from myself to me.

The aim of my book is to remind others that they are, simply enough, right here right now, just how and who they are. My book is to help others find self-worth and to accept all their imperfections, faults and mistakes and point out that you cannot change anything by dwelling in the past. Instead, live in the present moment with a clear mindset, letting go of any anger, hurt or pain that you carry around with you. That will never serve you and will only steal you from happiness. To find self-love and to focus more on what makes you happy, and all that you are grateful for, is always better than focusing on why others behave the way they do, or have what they have, because that is really none of your business, however, your own happiness, state of mind and well-being is.

I have learnt that it feels good not to think about anything that can or could go wrong, but to work on everything that could be going right. I always thought I was the most positive person ever because I had a lot of strength in naturally being a good soul and always being grateful and positive, but I've learnt that I grow and grow every day and that I am always learning and can always improve. We can often forget just how blessed we really are and how magical life really is and how anything is possible. Your state of mind is so important and I know they say your thoughts create your life but it's not just about that. It's not about never having feelings or emotions; it's about being ok with not feeling ok. It's about trying to balance life and trusting that all is good and that life does not have to be a struggle unless you choose it to be. It's about enjoying every moment, while trying to reach a goal and not complaining when things don't happen because they clearly aren't meant to be.

Why give up? Life isn't all plain sailing and the beauty of life is the pain, hurt and struggle that made you stronger and wiser, in order to move forward. If anything is handed to you on a plate, is it really worth it? Has it taught you what you need to learn? I've now learnt that questioning why isn't worth a thought, because we don't know why, we are all learning and we learn from our mistakes. To focus on our own actions and behaviour is much easier than wondering why others behave and act the way they do, because really it's their business and they are on their own path, like everyone else. Focus on you, because while you care what others are doing, you care less for yourself and have less time to work on yourself and that is never good, because self-love, self-worth and attention to oneself is most important and, with that, you feel good and feeling good puts you on a good vibration. With feeling good come good things, while feeling bad just makes things worse.

I want to talk about my visions, dreams and where my meditations take me. I dream a lot of white horses, rainbows, castles, bright flowers, loved ones and all that is love and light. Every night, once my boy goes to sleep, I lay in bed and can instantly go into meditation. As busy as my life is I can switch off really easily. It's not just once a week I have visions of rainbows and horses, it's most days and I believe it's leading me somewhere, trying to show me something. It's magical and I am very grateful for the visions which I believe come from my own thoughts and mindset.

I always seem to have white wings in my dreams and I fly a lot, I fly so high that I've hit rocks and broken my wings when I come down. I've fallen in rivers, flown across the bright blue sea and been dried off by the heat of the sunset. I've had wands with purple light coming from them while I have been waving them over people who need strength, hope, courage, confidence or just some guidance or understanding. I dream I'm flying, throwing out my book all over the world. All I want is for people to believe, I want people to know that if they clear their minds from trash they can have a vision of anything. I know I can and I know it's wonderful.

I know my life is so busy, yet I always take time to heal myself. I'm also aware that not everyone can help themselves. This is why I feel so blessed and thankful that I can. I feel so grateful for every second of my life and how every struggle has been a lesson and a blessing, how I've grown so much as a person and how believing in myself all my life has proved to me that magic really does exist and dreams really do come true. The most blessings I've found are the moment you are in and while it's ok to have goals, dreams and desires, it's also ok if you haven't touched them. As long as you can feel, from deep within, the joy of the journey, then I assure you your dreams will unfold for you.

People often ask me how I manage to think so positively and how I see the good in every single thing and person. The truth is that I live, breathe and feel blessed for every second of my life and not because I have it easy but because I choose not to make it hard, because life can be hard enough. People, situations and circumstances can be difficult if you choose to let other people's issues and insecurities be your problem. I've learnt to focus on me and my own issues so that I can grow, heal and love myself more than ever before. I found while trying to heal everyone else and trying to work out why others behave and treat you the way they do, I was draining myself and blocking any good feelings from coming in.

I now take care of myself and let others take care of themselves. Of course, I'm now more passionate than ever about wanting to help others but I've now learnt to protect my heart from being used, taken for granted or hurt, because I no longer care how others choose to treat me. I am aware they have their reasons and it's none of my business. I love myself deeply and feel blessed that I can help other people too. I just want to help people, I want people to know that they are not worthless, I want people to know that they can change the way they think and choose to feel, and that life does not have to feel like a struggle or a competition. I hate the thought of people thinking others are living happy lives and that they are not. I want people to know that life is, so simple and that we must be kind to ourselves, life does not have to be complicated we just choose to make it.

Walk in nature, gaze at the sky, think of flowers growing from seeds and blooming, gaze at the stars, feel energies, give love, receive love, see a new-born baby, hear the sound of a baby belly-laughing, smiling, talking, walking, singing and playing. Watch a baby's innocent soul grow and find joy in life. Learn to be grateful for literally everything, learn to love life without wanting things in return. I believe the universe and higher force works with you and guides you in the right direction for all the right reasons, I don't believe life is easy but I don't believe in making it harder for yourself either. We all experience loss, hurt and suffering and it's ok to wonder why, however, to force your anger, pain and frustration onto others is unfair as we need to understand that everything happens for a reason and that everything is ok and taken care of. Nobody knows why bad things happen but what I do know is that we are all stronger than we choose to think, and we are all loved, needed and thought of by someone. It is never good to dwell in self-pity feeling that you are a victim and that no one cares about you, because they do. The best thing to do is take care of yourself, love yourself and find so much self-worth that when life kicks you down, you just keep getting up, wiser, stronger, with more understanding and more love than ever before.

Allow yourself to grow and learn. Remember we are all human, and each and every one of us experiences just as much bad as good but our happiness depends on our attitude, behaviour, thoughts and actions, not our circumstance or situations. Please live, love and learn, then grow, blossom and bloom, and please be happy for those who choose happiness as they would have to have fought to become who they are today. Bring out the best in everyone you meet as your smile might make that person's day and your kind heart might warm someone else. We are all on our own journey and the beauty of life is so simple. We just fail to see or realise how blessed we really are.

So I am sitting here on a park bench and the sun is beaming on my face. I'm feeling so thankful for this glorious day, with an empty purse, but a heart full of love, I've never felt more blessed in my life. I have done so much walking since becoming a mum that I get joy from being soaked right through, I carry heavy bags and walk for miles because I refuse to pay for cabs or wait round for lifts. I've never appreciated nature more in all of my life. Losing my car has been a blessing, not a punishment. I power on without complaint. I feel like no one could ever understand me because I'm so grateful. I don't want people feeling sorry for me, I hear people complaining about such small things and I think that if I can get on with it then so can they.

I walk miles and miles, gazing at the stars, talking to the universe and asking my higher self to show me and guide me to what I was born to become. I see every day as being one step closer to what I came here to do and that is to write a best seller, then go on to write more books, to help others believe that they can too, and that life does not have to be a struggle - you can turn everything into a joy. Sulking gets you nowhere but getting up believing that you are enough is going to get you further or as far as you want to go; it is up to you.

I cannot begin to look back now. For me life is all about growth and choosing to better myself as a person, I won't waste any time on wondering why others behave, act and treat people the way they do. That is up to them and my life is up to me - I owe it to myself and I'm going to help so many people along the way. Since writing my book, I really have practiced what I preach more than ever before. I really have let go of so much of the weight I was carrying that I wasn't even aware of. I don't seem to let things bother me like I once did and I forgive and let go with so much ease.

It's as though I just know that nothing has to be a problem unless I choose to dwell on it, and if I can get through one bad day seeing only good, then I can get through another and every day can be beautiful. When it doesn't seem all that beautiful then that's also ok, because the next day will be better and, with every moment being grateful, I'm not thinking about what could go wrong. I'm just making room for good and all the new to come in, leaving my past where it is and focusing on the now and being happy in the moment. I no longer look or think of anything to dwell on and, any self-doubt I once had, I've let go of. I see only potential prosperity, abundance, health, wealth and happiness. I don't have time to think about why he or she said this or that, or behaves the way they do. I don't have time to wonder what they've got that I don't, or why I am nice and they are not - I do not care.

Working on myself brings me so much joy as does spending time doing things I love rather than focusing on why. I walk alone and it feels so good to be in my own thoughts. You have to love your own company and be your own best friend. It's something I've always been good at and the universe is really thanking me for it now and showing me things I've never really seen before.

For me, being grounded and good to others has always been my main goal in life, never forgetting were my bread is buttered and always keeping a grateful heart. If I want something, I make it happen, like a happy grateful day walking through nature, or parks or beaches or running through fields with my son breathing in life. We walk for miles, making magical memories, getting lost in the moment, and we always seem to have joyful days, splashing in puddles and kicking leaves, eating chip butties, waiting in train or bus stations naming all the transport colours and numbers. My little boy is so grateful and patient and nothing could buy that. I would never have been able to write my book if I didn't experience struggles. I'm not going to make out things come to me as easily but they do come, and my attitude, and strength have made me who I am today.

Before having my boy I worked day and night yet I've not been able to put every hour in since having my boy, as his happiness comes before everything. He gets every bit of me and if he's not happy then I'm not. He comes hairdressing with me and we walk and travel to every job through wind, hail and rain. We breathe in life and all its glory. Things work out for me because I choose not to complain and I'm consistent. Even when it's not always easy, I'm always grateful.

Chapter 12 - Note To Your Younger Self

Sweet child, I wish you wouldn't have covered your skin in plasters to cover your freckles, or felt you needed a tan in order to wear shorts in PE, or why you borrowed your friend's gymnastic swimsuit for swimming because it had long sleeves and you wanted to cover as much of your body as you could.

If only you could have loved the skin you're in as much as you do now.

Sweet child, if only you focused more on your dance lessons rather than caring that other people may see you getting the moves wrong; if only you knew then what you know now.

Although I have no regrets and would not change a thing, I'd still have believed sooner.

Sweet child, you really did do the best with what you had and still do. I've got to give you that. Working hard since leaving school and always passionate in everything you do.

You've always been so independent and ambitious. I admire how much you have grown in confidence, from a child to a girl to a woman, and now to a mother. I admire how much you have grown to find your passion and bring it to its purpose, but most of all to never stop believing when it's so easy to just give up. You've always kept going when times got hard. You've not complained, when people treat you wrongly you've easily forgiven and found the strength to not let it knock you.

When your world's felt like it's fallen apart, you've still seen the beauty in it. You've kept tight hold of your dreams and almost made them all a reality.

I really do love you and how you complain so very little even when you often want to break down and cry. You find a good in every bad and in all your insecurities you've found beliefs and never gave up.

You're always lifting others up when they don't have the time of day for yourself. You move on when you're feeling crushed, used, taken advantage of, powering on through pain when wanting to give up. When you're feeling in the dark you found light. You give love so freely without wanting anything in return.

I admire you for never giving up on your dreams and believing no matter how tough it's got, you make every second of your life count. I want to wish you all the health, wealth and happiness and only what you deserve, because I wouldn't change a thing – other than for you to see what I see and that's a beautiful, blessed child that deserves all the love and joy that life has to offer.

I believe in you, love, and admire you so much and how you walk your own path standing tall and proud, not wanting to fit in but doing what feels right not what looks good.

I love your uniqueness, your passion for life and people, your depth and how you strive every day to be a better you. I admire you for believing in you even if not a single other person does.

Epilogue

Five years ago I published a book called I BELIEVE IN ME. At the time, it seemed like the most incredible achievement of my life, because back then it was.

I thought I knew so much, only to realise that I didn't really know that much at all compared to what I know now. And I am still learning every single day.

It wasn't until my son started nursery at just 3 years old, and me being advised to put him in a special needs school because his brain wasn't developing as it should for a child his age. He was then put on a pathway and was referred to a special needs school. This woke me up like NEVER before, humbled me and changed my whole perception and outlook on life. This was to a point where I found myself having to let go of my whole identity after writing a book all about her, and walk through a whole new world with my son, in order to rebirth a brand new me.

Since publishing my first book, I have grown so much as a person and recently published a beautiful second book, five years later, called "You have nothing to prove". My son's journey with autism has transformed my life and myself as a person massively. I still believe this first book was a massive part of my growth, and if I hadn't have written it, then I never would have been lead to write this second book. I believe everything happens for a reason. It has been the most painful lessons, challenges and struggles that have pushed me to get both of my books published and available on Amazon, even though I didn't get a GCSE in school and failed in English. I still brought my dreams to life.

NEVER GIVE UP ON SOMETHING YOU DO NOT GO A DAY WITHOUT THINKING ABOUT, NEVER LET GO OF YOUR DREAMS, no matter how dark it may seem. Stay in your light, no matter what. REMEMBER that inner child you promised to make proud one day. Do it for her, push through your pain, BELIEVE IN YOURSELF and make your dreams your reality. It might get stormy, messy, challenging and painful, but do it anyway, follow your soul and listen to her, not the critics.

Life has taught me to massively let go of what we cannot control because while I believe that we create our own reality, I also believe some things happen that we have absolutely NO control over. LOVE, forgiveness and letting go heal EVERYTHING. SELF LOVE and GRATITUDE will save your life.

I believe that my first book may save people, it certainly won't harm ANYONE, just like my second book, as I come from a place of pure LOVE and good intention.

And as I learn, unlearn, relearn, as I grow and evolve, so shall you.

And if you would like to read my second book after this one, then you can get it on Amazon:

https://amzn.to/3jH7N3L

THANK YOU and ENJOY xx

Printed in Great Britain
by Amazon

68779121R00104